THE FOOD AND COOKING OF

SICILY

AND SOUTHERN ITALY

THE FOOD AND COOKING OF
SICILY
AND SOUTHERN ITALY

65 CLASSIC DISHES FROM SICILY, CALABRIA, BASILICATA AND PUGLIA

VALENTINA HARRIS

PHOTOGRAPHY BY MARTIN BRIGDALE

This edition is published by Aquamarine, an imprint of Anness Publishing Ltd, Hermes House, 88–89 Blackfriars Road, London SE1 8HA; tel. 020 7401 2077; fax 020 7633 9499

www.aquamarinebooks.com;
www.annesspublishing.com

If you like the images in this book and would like to investigate using them for publishing, promotions or advertising, please visit our website www.practicalpictures.com for more information.

UK agent: The Manning Partnership Ltd; tel. 01225 478444; fax 01225 478440; sales@manning-partnership.co.uk

UK distributor: Book Trade Services; tel. 0116 2759086; fax 0116 2759090; uksales@booktradeservices.com; exportsales@booktradeservices.com

North American agent/distributor: National Book Network; tel. 301 459 3366; fax 301 429 5746; www.nbnbooks.com

Australian agent/distributor: Pan Macmillan Australia; tel. 1300 135 113; fax 1300 135 103; customer.service@macmillan.com.au

New Zealand agent/distributor: David Bateman Ltd; tel. (09) 415 7664; fax (09) 415 8892

PUBLISHER'S NOTE
Although the advice and information in this book are believed to be accurate and true at the time of going to press, neither the authors nor the publisher can accept any legal responsibility or liability for any errors or omissions that may be made nor for any inaccuracies nor for any harm or injury that comes about from following instructions or advice in this book.

Publisher: Joanna Lorenz
Senior editor: Lucy Doncaster
Project editor: Kate Eddison
Copy editors: Catherine Best and Jan Cutler
Designer: Simon Daley
Photographer: Martin Brigdale
Food stylist: Valentina Harris
Prop stylist: Helen Trent
Illustrator: David Cook
Indexer: Diana LeCore
Proofreading Manager: Lindsay Zamponi
Editorial reader: Molly Perham
Production controller: Wendy Lawson

NOTES
Bracketed terms are intended for American readers. For all recipes, quantities are given in both metric and imperial measures and, where appropriate, in standard cups and spoons. Follow one set of measures, but not a mixture, because they are not interchangeable.
• Standard spoon and cup measures are level. 1 tsp = 5ml, 1 tbsp = 15ml, 1 cup = 250ml/8fl oz. Australian standard tablespoons are 20ml. Australian readers should use 3 tsp in place of 1 tbsp for measuring small quantities.
• American pints are 16fl oz/2 cups. American readers should use 20fl oz/2.5 cups in place of 1 pint when measuring liquids.
• Electric oven temperatures in this book are for conventional ovens. Using a fan oven, the temperature will probably need to be reduced by about 10–20°C /20–40°F. Since ovens vary, you should check with your manufacturer's instruction book for guidance.
• The nutritional analysis given for each recipe is calculated per portion (i.e. serving or item), unless otherwise stated. If the recipe gives a range, such as Serves 4–6, then the nutritional analysis will be for the smaller portion size, i.e. 6 servings.
• Measurements for sodium do not include salt added to taste.
• Medium (US large) eggs are used unless otherwise stated.

Front cover shows Home-made Pasta with Chickpeas – for recipe, see page 46.

A CIP catalogue record for this book is available from the British Library.

ETHICAL TRADING POLICY
At Anness Publishing we believe that business should be conducted in an ethical and ecologically sustainable way, with respect for the environment and a proper regard to the replacement of the natural resources we employ.

As a publisher, we use a lot of wood pulp to make high-quality paper for printing, and that wood commonly comes from spruce trees. We are therefore currently growing more than 750,000 trees in three Scottish forest plantations: Berrymoss (130 hectares/320 acres), West Touxhill (125 hectares/ 305 acres) and Deveron Forest (75 hectares/ 185 acres). The forests we manage contain more than 3.5 times the number of trees employed each year in making paper for the books we manufacture.

Because of this ongoing ecological investment programme, you, as our customer, can have the pleasure and reassurance of knowing that a tree is being cultivated on your behalf to naturally replace the materials used to make the book you are holding.

Our forestry programme is run in accordance with the UK Woodland Assurance Scheme (UKWAS) and will be certified by the internationally recognized Forest Stewardship Council (FSC). The FSC is a non-government organization dedicated to promoting responsible management of the world's forests. Certification ensures forests are managed in an environmentally sustainable and socially responsible way. For further information about this scheme, go to www.annesspublishing.com/trees

CONTENTS

A SUN-BAKED LANDSCAPE

The hot and arid regions of Sicily, Calabria, Basilicata and Puglia lie in the sun-drenched south of Italy, and are part of the Mezzogiorno, which also includes Molise and Campania. Long expanses of coastline plunge into the temperate waters of the Mediterranean, but inland, mysterious forests, rugged mountains and ancient villages provide startling natural beauty too. On a map, Italy resembles a boot kicking a ball. With this in mind, the four regions of southern Italy are easy to identify: Puglia is the heel, Basilicata is the instep, Calabria is the toe and Sicily is the ball. The whole of southern Italy is rich in history, culture, art and gastronomy; but it is so different from the industrial north that it is sometimes hard to believe it is part of the same country.

The south of Italy has a typical Mediterranean climate, with short, mild, wet winters and long, hot, dry summers with only occasional rain and thunderstorms. Summers in the south are mainly influenced by the Sirocco, an incredibly hot wind from the North African coast. The scorching temperatures are the dominating feature of the whole area, especially during the summer, when the ground turns into parched dust, although it can also become extremely cold in winter up in the highest mountains. Despite the heat and aridity, these regions produce legendary wines, a vast cornucopia of wonderful fruit and vegetables, and fields of golden durum wheat for making world-famous pasta and delicious bread.

SICILY – AN ISLAND OF NATURAL BEAUTY
A truly amazing island, Sicily is set like a jewel in the blue waters of three seas. It is a place of breathtaking natural beauty, with rugged hills, rocky inlets, wide sandy beaches and Etna, the stupendous volcano that dominates the land. The architectural

and agricultural legacy of the various nations who have ruled here, from the Phoenicians, Greeks and Romans to the Arabs and Spanish, still remain.

The warm climate and an almost total absence of frost allows Sicilian farmers to grow tender crops. Never-ending groves of citrus fruits and olives and sprawling vines bearing watermelons and grapes are visible at every turn. The best weather is usually found near the coast – inland and in the larger cities it can be unbearably hot. The southern and western coasts are, however, close to Africa and therefore susceptible to higher temperatures and the Sirocco wind.

CALABRIA – A MOUNTAINOUS REGION
Across the Strait of Messina, where the narrowest strip of sea between Sicily and the mainland is only 3.2km (2 miles) wide, lies the region of Calabria. Two deep furrows running east to west divide the landscape into three mountainous sections. This natural formation tends to isolate the towns and cities from each other.

BELOW *Sicily, Calabria, Basilicata and Puglia are set at the very south of Italy, in the warm waters of the Mediterranean.*

BELOW RIGHT *South Italy, set close to the North African coast, experiences a hot, dry climate.*

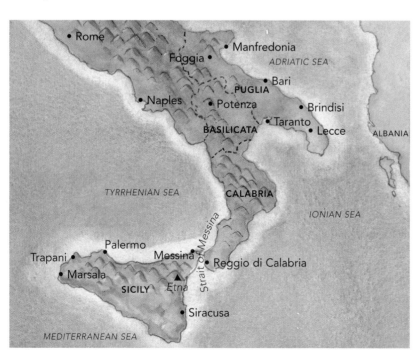

The Pollino Mountains in the north of the region form a natural barrier separating Calabria from the rest of Italy. Some parts are heavily wooded, while others are windswept plateaus with little vegetation or agriculture. La Sila, in the centre, is a vast mountainous plateau about 1,200m (4,000ft) above sea level, which boasts numerous lakes and dense coniferous forests, and is famous for the production of cheeses. The southern Aspromonte range overlooks the Straits of Messina. The rare bergamot, a lemony-yellow fruit used in perfumes and to flavour Earl Grey tea, flourishes here, but agriculture in Calabria is mainly limited to the level areas near the coast, where citrus fruits, vegetables, vines and olives grow profusely, and tender, valuable crops such as sugar beet, tobacco, flowers and oranges abound, as well as fig and almond trees. Sheep farming, though very traditional all over this region, is sadly in decline.

BASILICATA – A RUGGED TERRAIN

The 'instep' of the Italian 'boot', Basilicata has little coastline compared to the other southern regions – it has one short coastline on the Tyrrhenian Sea to the west and another on the Gulf of Taranto to the south-east. Set at the southern end of the Apennine mountain range, which runs down the spine of Italy, the region is almost entirely mountainous and the harsh terrain has always made communications difficult. This is a land of farmers and shepherds, who tend their hardy flocks on the stony slopes of the mountains. Until very recent times Basilicata was one of the least developed provinces of Italy, and one of its poorest regions, but the area has become significantly richer over the past years, largely thanks to the recent discovery of oil under the rocks.

PUGLIA – THE LOWLANDS

This region, known as Apulia in English, is located in the eastern tip of the Italian peninsula. It has the longest continuous stretch of coastline of any region of Italy, and near the beautiful resort area of the Gargano are Italy's largest coastal lakes – Lesina and Varano. The landscape of the region consists of flat plains and soft hills, which are ideal for food production in the warm climate. Puglia is more economically developed than other southern regions, and a range of crops are grown here, including durum wheat, figs, tobacco and sugar beet. The fields also contain rows of lettuce, peppers, fennel, artichokes, grapes, almonds and olives. Pugliese olive oil is famous the world over, and is reputed to have been Cleopatra's favourite oil. Sheep farming is a longstanding tradition, and fishing thrives along the length of the coastline.

ABOVE LEFT *The sparkling blue waters of the Tyrrhenian Sea provide a dazzling backdrop to the Calabrian coastline.*

ABOVE *A farmer ploughs the rugged, arid landscape of the Gargano in Puglia.*

BELOW *The wonderfully preserved ancient Greek theatre in Taormina on the east coast of Sicily sits in a remarkably picturesque location, with views over Mount Etna.*

A TURBULENT HISTORY

The south of Italy followed a different historical path from the north. After hundreds of years of Roman domination, the southern regions were fought over in constant battles between the Greeks, Lombards and Caliphs, to name a few. The area became part of Spain until Duke Victor Amadeus II of Sardinia took Sicily in 1713. The south was eventually conquered by Giuseppe Garibaldi and the Redshirts in 1861 and, with the north, formed the modern State of Italy. The landscape of the south is rich with evidence of a turbulent, diverse and fascinating history – it is dotted with ancient Greek temples and amphitheatres, beautiful Roman mosaics, enduring Byzantine architecture and splendid Norman churches.

SICILY – PLAYTHING OF FOREIGN POWERS

Colonized by the Greeks from the 8th century BC, Sicily was included as part of Magna Graecia. However, by 242BC, Sicily was in Roman hands, becoming Rome's first province outside the Italian peninsula. For the next six centuries Sicily remained something of a rural backwater, prized chiefly for its golden fields of grain, which were a mainstay of the food supply for the Roman population.

In AD826, an Islamic army of Arabs, Berbers, Spaniards, Cretans and Persians was sent to Sicily. The conquest took over a century to be completed, with Syracuse holding out for a long time, but the island was finally conquered in AD965. During this period, new kinds of crops, such as oranges, lemons, pistachios and sugar cane, were brought to Sicily from North Africa.

Over the next millennium, Sicily was continuously fought over by the Normans, Lombards, French, Spanish and various other royal houses of Europe. Even when Italy as a country was finally unified, Sicily, and much of southern Italy, was the object of harsh repression by the Italian army. The Sicilian economy did not adapt easily to unification, and competition with northern industrial giants made industrialization in the south very difficult.

CALABRIA – A GROWING ECONOMY

Like Sicily, Calabria was part of the rich and powerful Magna Graecia, until the Romans conquered it. Throughout the millennium that followed the fall of the Roman Empire, Calabria too was occupied by a multitude of invading forces. During these periods the population, plagued by malaria epidemics as well as violent raids by the Saracens and the Turks along the coast, withdrew to the mountains. This phenomenon created an internal and external isolation, with the population of each valley often unable to visit the next because of impassable roads during the winter. When Italy was unified in 1861, Calabria had only one road that crossed it from the north coast to Reggio in the south, and there was no railway.

The efforts of the national government and Mussolini's regime in the 20th century contributed to breaking this isolation. More recently, social and

BELOW LEFT *This 12th-century Byzantine mosaic from La Martorana church in Palermo, Sicily, depicts Christ crowning King Roger II of Sicily (1093–1154).*

BELOW RIGHT *This illustration shows the 11th-century Norman fleet of Roger de Hautville, who conquered Puglia and Calabria, and destroyed the Saracen fleet at Palermo.*

economic conditions have changed radically. Thanks to tourism, towns have sprung up along the coast, packed with restaurants serving the delicious specialities of the region.

BASILICATA – A NEGLECTED REGION

In Roman times Basilicata was known as Lucania, after the Lucani people who were the first known invaders of the region before the Greeks invaded during the 7th century BC. The area was under Roman rule by the 2nd century BC and under the government of Rome it fell into decay. Cities on the coast became depopulated, and malaria began to gain the upper hand. The few towns of the interior were of little importance. A large part of the land was given over to pasture, and the mountains were covered with forests, which were full of wild boar, bears and wolves. In more recent times, the discovery of oil within the harsh mountainous landscape has meant the region has started to regenerate and has begun to promote its emerging tourist industry.

PUGLIA – A TREASURED FOOD STORE

One of the richest areas in Italy in terms of archaeology, this region was inhabited from the 1st millennium BC, and like most of the south, it formed part of the Magna Graecia. Later, the Romans captured the ports of Brindisi and Taranto, and established their domination. During Roman occupation, Puglia was renowned for its grain and olive oil, becoming the most important exporter of these ingredients to the eastern provinces. Top-quality durum wheat, which makes delicious bread and pasta, remains its main crop to this day.

After the fall of Rome, Puglia was held successively by the Goths, the Lombards and, from the 6th century onward, the Byzantines. From AD800 the region was mostly under Byzantine authority, and subsequently, like much of the south, it was controlled by different European powers whose various influences can be seen in the architecture. In 1861 the region of Puglia finally joined the State of Italy.

COPING WITH ORGANIZED CRIME

Government neglect in the 19th century ultimately enabled the establishment of an organized crime network commonly known as La Mafia, with influence in many areas of Sicilian culture, not least in food production and restaurants. Efforts to eradicate it in Italy and the USA continue to this day.

ABOVE *This majestic ancient Greek temple in Segesta, in the province of Trapani, is a reminder of Sicily's rich history.*

A VIBRANT CUISINE

The differences between the south of Italy, especially the far south, and the north are highlighted in its food traditions. Pasta here means dried pasta, as opposed to the fresh home-made pasta and hearty polenta of the northern regions, and meat and cheese are eaten only in small quantities. A hot climate with relentless sunshine, slow industrialization and myriad historical influences has led to the cuisine of the south being generally earthy and peasant-like with exotic twists of taste. Compared to the north, the flavours are stronger and the combinations of ingredients are bolder, which mirrors the extremes of the climate and landscape, and perhaps also the hot-blooded nature of the people.

BELOW *Caciocavallo, a Sicilian cheese made with cow's milk, is still made in the traditional way.*

THE CUISINE OF SICILY

This small island off Italy's south-western coast is a living celebration of family, food and culture. The landscape, a mosaic of golden coastlines and wheat fields, fruit orchards, lush forests, flourishing vineyards and brilliant wild flowers, has inspired works of art in writing, painting and cuisine. The legacy of the island's many invaders throughout history – Romans, Byzantines, Arabs, Normans and Spaniards – has fostered a fascinating multicultural cuisine full of exotic and aromatic dishes. A culinary tour of Sicily is always a joy.

Savoury delights A Sicilian meal might start with caponata, an appetizer made of aubergine (eggplant), pine nuts, celery, olives and capers. The recipe varies, sometimes including artichokes and even chocolate. To the west, in Palermo, the aroma of Arab-inspired vegetable couscous and roast lamb made with herbs and spices wafts from the town's jostling open-air markets. Down by the southern coast, fish, mussels and clams, which have been plucked from the Mediterranean, are for sale on the quayside. The most famous cheese of the region is Caciocavallo, which is made from curdled cow's milk.

THE MEDITERRANEAN DIET

Researchers have discovered that people in the countries bordering the Mediterranean Sea, especially southern Italy, exhibit strikingly low rates of heart disease compared with Americans or Northern Europeans. Meals consist of grains, fruits, pulses and vegetables, with a little meat, cheese and fish. The main fat is olive oil, which is used in lavish quantities instead of butter. The garlic that appears in many dishes may help prevent blood clots, lower cholesterol and protect against cancer. The Mediterranean diet also includes moderate amounts of red wine, which may help protect the heart.

Sweet treats Ice cream is almost a Sicilian obsession. An abundance of flavours and varieties are available, including the very special granita al caffè con panna, a slushy iced coffee topped with whipped cream.

Among the vast array of sweetmeats in a Sicilian pastry shop window, the place of honour definitely goes to the cassata. Made of a tantalizing mixture of sponge cake, chocolate, sweetened ricotta cheese, candied fruit and nuts, cassata is usually decorated with thick icing or marzipan and covered with more brightly coloured candied fruits. The ever-popular cannoli, deep-fried pastry cylinders filled with a rich combination of sweetened ricotta, chocolate and candied fruit, were once a treat only at carnival time, but are now enjoyed all year round.

Centuries ago, a delicious sweet wine was created in the western Sicilian town of Marsala to challenge the Portuguese and Spanish monopoly on fortified wines such as Madeira and sherry. Today, Marsala is used all over the world to enhance the flavour of a dish, as part of a sauce, or to be sipped as a dessert wine.

THE CUISINE OF CALABRIA

Although it is neither refined nor rich in ingredients, the cuisine of Calabria is very substantial and infused with the intense flavours of chilli peppers, mint, garlic, tomatoes, sweet (bell) peppers, aubergines and the famous red onions of Tropea. Durum wheat pasta, pork and bread, as well as fish

ABOVE *A shepherd leads his sheep through hilly farmland in Calabria.*

in the coastal areas, are the key foods enjoyed by Calabrians. The region boasts a strong, frugal peasant tradition that combines simple ingredients to make lively, tasty foods.

Inventiveness and thrift One of the dishes that sums up the Calabrian philosophy of food is caviale dei poveri (poor people's caviar), made by packing herring roe in oil and flavouring it with hot chilli peppers. Bottarga, or preserved tuna roe, is another local speciality and features prominently in many traditional dishes.

The sheep that scramble over the rocks are the source of delicious lamb dishes and many different cheeses made with ewe's milk. Vegetables of all kinds abound, and fiery chilli peppers are used to spice up everything from cured meats to pasta. Particularly famous are the Calabrian soft chilli-flavoured sausages, which are served as appetizers or in sandwiches.

Figs, chestnuts and almonds are mainly used in desserts such as fichi ripieni (stuffed figs), a speciality of Cosenza that tops dried figs with cocoa, almonds and other nuts. These few sweet ingredients are essential to local cooking and form the basis of many dishes.

PRESERVING FOOD

Calabrians have traditionally placed a great emphasis on preserving their foods, partly because the dry, hot climate of the mountains inland makes crop failures a distinct possibility. For this reason, the Calabrian people plan ahead, bottling vegetables and meats in oil, salting meat and, along the coast, curing fish, especially swordfish and tuna.

LEFT *A wine-maker takes a sample of sweet Marsala Superiore from casks in Sicily where it is aged for at least two years.*

A farmer in Basilicata begins to reap the golden fields of durum wheat.

THE CUISINE OF BASILICATA

With little coastline and a mountainous, rugged interior, Basilicata is a rural farming region, so pork, pasta (simply made from durum wheat and water), bread and vegetables are the stars of the table. The flavours of the local food are always robust, sharp and intense. Desserts are also good, especially those sweetened with the local honey.

A peasant cuisine Pork is the fundamental staple food. A pig can be reared in any kind of terrain and every bit can be used, even its blood, which is used for making a well-known local dessert called sanguinaccio. These pigs are generally muscular, and yield a ham that is dry, sinewy and full of flavour, especially when cured with wonderful spices. The famous pork sausage of Basilicata is made using only top-quality pork seasoned with fennel seeds, salt and pepper, or peperoncino.
This sausage has a strong and aggressive taste, and is eaten fresh, roasted, fried, smoked and left to dry, or preserved in oil. Other local sausages include soppressata, a dry-cured salami, and the typical pezzente (beggar), a sausage composed of meat scraps chopped up into tiny pieces and

flavoured with generous quantities of pepper and garlic. Another very typical dish of the Basilicata region is lamb, mutton or kid cooked in a pignata, or deep earthenware pot.

Bread is absolutely vital to the cuisine of Basilicata. Durum wheat is the basis of both bread and pasta, and has been cultivated here since time immemorial. Bread appears not only as an accompaniment to meals, but also as a basis for many dishes, sitting at the bottom of a bowl of salad or soup, for example, to provide bulk.

CHILLI PEPPERS

Beneath the tranquil surface of Basilicata's quiet exterior lies a cuisine that rages with the heat of the peperoncino, the fiery chilli pepper that is found in all sorts of shapes and sizes at the local markets. The 'little red devil' is used in such generous quantities in Basilicata that the unsuspecting tourist, as well as the uninitiated Italian, may find themselves gasping for breath and reaching for a cooling drink.

Pasta shapes of all kinds are made using just durum wheat flour, water and salt, kneaded and shaped by hand to produce dough that is much thicker than industrially made dry pasta. The most common dressing for pasta in Basilicata is a tomato and meat sauce with small pieces of mutton or lamb, which have been sliced with a knife, rather than minced (ground). On top of the meat sauce, there will be a sprinkling of strong cheese as well as chilli pepper fried in oil. Bright and fragrant, this is a substantial pasta dish.

THE CUISINE OF PUGLIA

Puglia overflows with the fruits of both land and sea. It has golden wheat fields, plentiful olive groves, famous vineyards, and good fishing grounds in the Adriatic and Ionian Sea. The dry, hot climate makes it ideal for growing top-quality durum wheat – accounting for the superior, irresistible taste of its bread and pasta – and producing world-renowned olive oil. With good cheer and hospitality, delicious food and wine, a Pugliese feast is always a memorable experience.

Simple tastes of the countryside Puglia cultivates most types of wheat, but durum wheat is the main crop. The density of this wheat, combined with its high protein content and gluten strength, make it the best choice for producing fantastic pasta and bread. Pane di Altamura is a wonderful sourdough bread, made only with durum wheat flour from the Alta Murgia near Bari, plus natural yeast, water and salt. It is shaped into enormous round loaves and baked in ovens fired by oak wood. When freshly baked, it is soft on the inside with a crunchy coat, becoming firmer after a few days.

Shellfish is very popular in this region, especially in the area around Bari where the locals love to eat it raw, freshly plucked from the sea. Broad (fava) beans, tomatoes, aubergine (eggplant), broccoli and courgettes (zucchini) are just a few of the exquisite vegetables cultivated in the region's rich, fertile soil.

Most of the cakes and desserts found in Puglia are very sweet, based on almonds, sugar and sometimes honey as well. There is a great tradition in this region of making desserts for special occasions, and these tend to be wonderfully elaborate confections in comparison to the simpler everyday sweetmeats, cakes and biscuits (cookies).

OLIVE OIL

The different varieties of olive oil produced in Puglia are regarded as some of the finest olive oils in the world. For a simple taste of Puglia, tear off a generous piece of local rustic bread, such as pane di Altamura, and dip it into one of the many provincial varieties of olive oil to enjoy the splendid range and intensity of flavour.

BELOW LEFT *Fiery chilli peppers are hung out to dry in the scorching Basilicata sun.*

BELOW RIGHT *Vibrantly coloured lemon groves overflowing with ripe fruit are ready to be harvested in Sicily.*

FESTIVALS AND CELEBRATIONS

One of the best ways to get to know a country is through its festivals. While this often means braving crowds of boisterous people, especially in the south, it also means enjoying the food and drink of the region at its flamboyant best. In southern Italy it seems as if there is always some town or village in the region that is in party mode, with saint's days, celebrations of particular seasonal foods or dishes, sporting events and much more.

CHRISTMAS AND EPIPHANY
In southern Italy, Christmas is traditionally celebrated right through from 24 December, Christmas Eve, to 6 January, Epiphany. This Christian festival was originally based on the pagan season that started with Saturnalia, a winter solstice festival, and ended on the Roman New Year, the Calends. Traditional Christmas food includes a selection of fish dishes on Christmas Eve, when meat is shunned, and a long lunch of several courses on Christmas Day. For sweet treats, southern Italians love panettone and cookies served with figs and plenty of sugar.

NEW YEAR
La Festa di San Silvestro is celebrated on 31 December, New Year's Eve. As with most Italian festivals, food plays a major role, and families and friends get together for a huge feast. The star of the dinner is a dish of lentils, representing money and good fortune. Traditionally, the dinner also includes cotechino, a large spiced sausage, or zampone, stuffed pig's trotters. These pork dishes symbolize the richness of life that is wished for the coming year.

Most towns have huge midnight firework displays in a central square. Parties will often last until dawn so that the guests can watch the first sunrise of the newborn year together.

> **THE CHRISTMAS WITCH**
>
> Although Babbo Natale (Father Christmas) and Christmas presents are becoming more common, the tradition of La Befana is still a big part of Christmas celebrations. This is the tale of a white-haired witch who arrives on her broomstick during the night of 5 January and fills the children's stockings with toys and sweets for the well-behaved and lumps of coal for the naughty ones.

An old custom that is still followed in some southern towns is to throw old possessions, from china to furniture, out of the window to symbolize a readiness to embrace the new year with a fresh start.

FESTIVAL OF SAINT AGATHA
This celebration takes place during 3–5 February in Catania, Sicily, to honour the life of Saint Agatha of Sicily. Among other things, she is the patron saint of bakers, whose loaves are blessed on the feast day.

CARNIVAL
This is a huge winter festival in Italy, celebrated with parades, masquerade balls, entertainments, music, food and parties. Children throw confetti at each

BELOW LEFT A solemn procession takes place during Holy Week in the village of Leonforte, Sicily.

BELOW RIGHT A Sicilian bride and her father walk along the cobbled streets of Taormina.

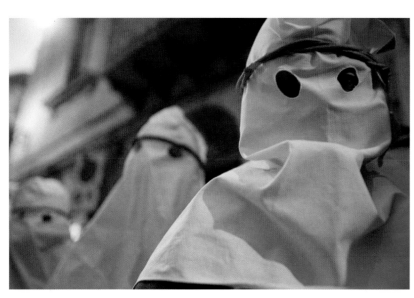

other, and mischief and pranks are common, hence the saying: 'a carnevale ogni scherzo vale' (anything goes at carnival).

Carnival has its roots in pagan traditions and, as is often the case with traditional festivals, was adapted to fit into Catholic rituals. Some carnival traditions in Sicily date back to the 17th century, including the construction of the first papier-mâché chariot in Palermo in 1601, which represented Neptune surrounded by mermaids. This art form was then adopted by other towns in Sicily with great enthusiasm. The food tends to be rich and fatty, with pork being the favourite meat. Carnival is followed swiftly by a period of self-restraint in Lent.

LENT

Catholics traditionally abstain from certain rich foods for the 40 days before Easter, both as penance for their sins, and to reflect on Jesus' crucifixion and resurrection. Today, many Italians still make sacrifices or changes to their lives during Lent. The most well-known rule is meatless Fridays, when people eat fish and vegetables instead of meat. Indeed, some Italian Catholics refrain from eating meat on Fridays all year round, but this is a personal choice and no longer a Church rule.

EASTER

Solemn religious processions are held in many towns on the Friday or Saturday before Easter and sometimes also on Easter Sunday. Olive branches and palm fronds are waved and used to decorate the churches. Among the many desserts and cakes eaten during the Easter period, the most traditional is scarcedda from Basilicata. This has a pastry base filled with ricotta cheese, and hidden inside is a peeled hard-boiled egg. Whoever finds the egg (or a piece of it) in their slice will have a lucky year.

FEAST OF SAN PAOLO

This popular feast is celebrated in the town of Palazzolo Acreide, Sicily, 27–29 June. On the feast day, large, doughnut-shaped loaves of bread are offered to the saint, as well as being sold to festival goers, to celebrate the harvest of a good wheat crop.

AUTUMN FESTIVAL

The slaughtering of a pig in November has become a ceremony that is tied to legends, customs and traditions. The festival climax is at the dinner table where an exceptionally rich meal of pork is served. The remaining pig is made into delicious sausages and cured meats to last the next few months.

FAMILY CELEBRATIONS

Baptisms, first communions and weddings are among the most important celebrations for families in southern Italy. No expense is spared, from the clothes to the venue and menu. These enormous feasts, to which hundreds of family members and friends are invited, are opportunities for people to show off their wealth and generosity. It is considered dishonourable to provide anything less than a huge banquet, however much it costs.

ABOVE LEFT *Musicians perform at the Sagra del Mandorlo in Fiore, a celebration of folk dance and music, where Sicilian farmers promote local products each spring.*

ABOVE RIGHT *Bread is distributed in Palazzolo Acreide, Sicily, during the feast of San Paolo.*

CLASSIC INGREDIENTS

The flavours of southern Italy have nothing subtle about them. This is food that has an almost aggressive effect on the palate, whether it is ultra-sweet, spicy or savoury. Cooks make the most of the simple ingredients that manage to thrive in the hot, dry climate, such as olives, chilli peppers, durum wheat, fresh seasonal fruits, vegetables, herbs and nuts. Meat and cheese are used sparingly, unlike in the northern regions, but fresh fish and shellfish form an important element of the cuisine due to the extensive coastlines of each region. An array of refreshing ingredients are turned into cooling ice creams and sorbets, and a glass of full-bodied wine or a sweet liqueur are an essential part of the daily southern diet.

FISH AND SHELLFISH

The regions with the longest coastlines – Puglia, Calabria and Sicily – have the strongest fish cuisines. All kinds of sea fish and shellfish are caught in season. Varieties such as cod that thrive in colder waters further north are eaten in their dried and salted form, baccalà, a much-loved delicacy.

For hundreds of years, fishermen have captured the Mediterranean bluefin tuna every May and June as they migrate past the coast. They are eaten fresh in season with a simple tomato sauce. The swordfish season is longer, from May to October; the flesh is sturdy and well-flavoured, perfect for baking in the oven. Anchovies and sardines are served fresh, as well as being salted and preserved in olive oil. Solid, meaty fish, such as red mullet, bream and John Dory, are all caught in these warm waters and make delicious main courses or mixed fish soup.

Mussels and other kinds of shellfish are especially popular in Puglia, where they are often eaten raw. Elsewhere in the south they are more likely to be cooked, especially in sauces for pasta. Fresh, raw sea urchins are also enjoyed in many coastal areas.

MEAT

Beef, chicken and veal are rare in southern cuisine, although beef is now becoming more common. Traditional recipes focus more on pork, lamb, goat

> ### A RICH BREAKFAST
>
> Some Calabrians enjoy a hearty cooked breakfast dish called murseddu – a ragù made from pig's and calf's liver, simmered with tomatoes, herbs and hot red peppers, stuffed into the local pitta bread.

BELOW, LEFT TO RIGHT
Fresh mussels, tuna steaks, pancetta and Provola cheese.

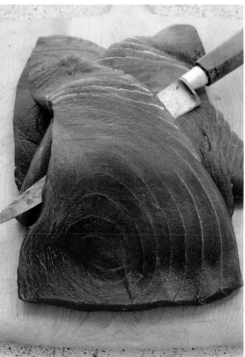

and mutton. In fact, the typical Mediterranean diet of the region means that meat is often reserved for special occasions. Pork sausages and cured meats, however, are popular, and rendered pork fat is used both as a preservative and as a cooking fat, especially in the winter months. Pancetta, or bacon, is used in small quantities in many recipes, bringing a luxurious flavour to even the most simple dish. In Basilicata and Puglia, lamb, goat and mutton offal (innards) are delicacies.

DAIRY PRODUCTS

With little dairy farming in this mountainous region, most of the superb cheeses are made of sheep's milk, such as the wonderfully rich Burrata (a kind of enormous mozzarella with a buttery centre). Other popular sheep's milk cheeses include Pecorino, Caciocavallo and Primosale. Ricotta forte, a speciality of Matera and Puglia, is a version of the well-known soft cheese, seasoned daily for 30 days, gradually becoming saltier and more intense in flavour. It is spread on bread, or spooned on top of pizzas, pasta and soup.

VEGETABLES

A fabulous variety of fresh vegetables are grown in southern Italy. The sun develops their sweet flavours so that they can be eaten raw or cooked, or preserved in oil for the cooler winter. The dry heat and nearly calcium-free soil give ideal conditions for growing aubergines (eggplants), (bell) peppers and courgettes (zucchini) with no trace of bitterness.

RAGÙ

SERVES 4 (ENOUGH FOR 400G/14OZ DRIED PASTA)

25g/1oz dried porcini mushrooms (optional)
90ml/6 tbsp olive oil or vegetable oil
1 onion, finely chopped
2 celery sticks, finely chopped
1 carrot, finely chopped
1 garlic clove, finely chopped
50g/2oz fat prosciutto crudo or streaky (fatty) bacon, finely chopped
450g/1lb/2 cups lean minced (ground) beef
200ml/7fl oz/scant 1 cup red wine
15ml/1 tsp tomato purée (paste) diluted with 90ml/6 tbsp warm water
400g/14oz passata (bottled strained tomatoes) or canned tomatoes
sea salt and ground black pepper

1 If using the porcini, soak them in warm water to cover for 15 minutes, then drain. Discard the stems and slice the caps.

2 Heat the oil in a large, heavy pan and fry the onion, celery, carrot and garlic together for 5 minutes until the onion is soft and transparent. Add the prosciutto or bacon, stir and cook over low heat for 4 minutes more.

3 Add the porcini (if using) and the beef. Raise the heat to medium and brown the beef carefully, without letting it go crisp, then pour in the wine and raise the heat to the maximum to evaporate the alcohol.

4 Pour in the diluted tomato purée and the passata or canned tomatoes. Stir carefully, season to taste, lower the heat and cover.

5 Simmer very very slowly for about 2 hours, stirring frequently and adding water or stock if the mixture becomes too thick. Serve with spaghetti.

L'ARRABIATA

This hot, spicy sauce tastes great with pasta, and also makes a marvellous dipping sauce. Try it with Sicilian Mushroom Fritters.

SERVES 4 (ENOUGH FOR 400G/14OZ DRIED PASTA)

60ml/4 tbsp extra virgin olive oil
4 garlic cloves, finely chopped
1–4 dried red chillies (see Cook's Tips)
2 x 397g/14oz cans chopped tomatoes, drained
sea salt
5ml/1 tsp chopped fresh parsley, to serve

1 Heat the olive oil in a large, heavy pan and add the garlic and chilli(es).

2 Fry for 3–4 minutes until both the garlic and chilli(es) are well browned.

3 Remove the chilli(es) and garlic with a slotted spoon and discard them.

4 Add the tomatoes to the pan and season with salt.

5 Simmer for 20 minutes, until the sauce is thick and flavoursome.

6 Whether you serve l'arrabiata with cooked pasta or as a dipping sauce, sprinkle with the chopped parsley when serving.

Cook's Tips
• The number of chillies that you use depends upon their strength as well as how hot you want the sauce to be. To achieve maximum heat, include the seeds.
• Cheese is not normally served when l'arrabiata is part of a dish, but if you or your guests insist on having cheese, it has to be aged, peppery Pecorino.

In Calabria, the aubergine (eggplant) has been the queen of vegetables for centuries and features as a substantial main ingredient in baked dishes. Sweet (bell) peppers come in green, yellow or red, and the huge, heavy varieties grown in Calabria are particularly prized. In Sicily, artichokes are baked whole in the core of a wood fire, then dressed with lemon juice, olive oil and salt to make a deliciously simple treat. Wild mushrooms of many different kinds grow abundantly in the woods and forests of Calabria and Basilicata. They can be dried for later use, which preserves them and also intensifies the flavour.

Salad vegetables include cucumber, which is a staple of the dinner table in Sicily, especially the unusual small round type. Countless varieties of tasty tomatoes are used as an ingredient or in salads or as an accompanying vegetable all over the southern regions. They are also sun-dried and bottled for use throughout the winter as well as for making the thick, dark red Sicilian tomato paste known as strattu.

LAMPASCIONI – A SOUTHERN CURIOSITY

These vegetables are actually wild hyacinth bulbs, distant relatives of the garlic plant, and resemble a small onion. They can be cooked in the embers of a fire, then peeled and seasoned with oil, vinegar and salt. They taste very bitter to the uninitiated, but are adored by the locals.

Olives of various sizes and colours are widely used for cooking, as well as for eating as a snack or as an appetizer, and olive oil is one of the defining ingredients of the food of southern Italy. Much less peppery than olive oil from Tuscany, it is generally sweet and thick, and is used liberally to cook and dress all the local savoury dishes.

Pulses such as beans, lentils, dried broad (fava) beans and chickpeas are all on the menu, providing bulk and excellent nutritious qualities. Chickpeas sometimes even appear in sweet dishes or as part of a pasta dough.

FRUIT AND NUTS

Citrus fruits grow happily in the hot sun of the south. The cuisine would be unthinkable without lemons, and the juice, zest, whole peel and even leaves of this fruit are used in recipes every day. The tarrocco orange, or blood orange, with its dark blood-red colour, is grown in Sicily alongside the paler varieties. The Sicilian lime is large and knobbly, with an enormous amount of skin and

---

PRICKLY PEAR

The dangerous-looking fruit of the flat-leaved cactus plant, prickly pear, is considered a real delicacy in Sicily and is grown mainly in the area around San Cono. These fruits are yellow, orange and red in colour, and are only slightly sweet in flavour, with lots of seeds.

---

pith surrounding the juicy flesh buried in the centre. It makes a sweet cordial called Cedrata, and beautiful candied peel for use in pastries.

Many other fruits grow on the warm hillsides of southern Italy, including plums, apricots, cherries and peaches, and are eaten fresh or pulped for fruit cordials. Purple mulberries make the most delicious ice cream. Black and green figs are eaten fresh, baked in cakes and pastries, made into jam, dried, or stuffed with nuts and coated with chocolate.

Almonds are used in countless savoury and sweet dishes in these regions, and the milk squeezed from the fresh nuts is turned into a cooling drink mixed with sugar and water. Pistachio nuts are very typical of the island of Sicily and grow especially well on the lower slopes of Mount Etna. They are largely used in cooking, especially in desserts and ice cream.

HERBS AND SEASONINGS

Oregano is a sharp, tangy herb that lends its very special flavour, in dried form, to many dishes of the south. Flat leaf parsley is used as a garnish, as much for its colour and fragrance as for its flavour. In Sicily, the tiny-leaved variety of basil is most commonly used in everything from meatballs to pasta sauces. The green fronds of wild fennel are the key ingredient in the famous pasta dish of Sicily, pasta con le sarde.

Other key flavourings include capers, which are especially prized in the cooking of southern Italy. These tiny green buds add a note of acidity to

ABOVE, LEFT TO RIGHT
Artichokes, yellow pepper, dried white broad beans and mixed candied fruits.

many dishes, such as pasta sauces. The strong flavour of garlic also permeates southern Italian cooking. One of the most important ingredients in the culinary heritage of Calabria and Basilicata is the chilli pepper, which adds its fiery heat to most savoury dishes.

Spices such as cinnamon, cumin, nutmeg, ground coriander and fennel seeds are undoubtedly a legacy of the Arab domination of Sicily. Bergamot oranges thrive only in Calabria, and their essential oil is used to flavour liqueurs, teas (such as Earl Grey), sweets and drinks, and also in perfumery and cosmetics.

GRAINS

These warm southern Italian regions are ideal for growing the hard durum wheat that makes the finest quality bread and pasta. The skill lies in the blending, kneading and shaping of the basic ingredients: wheat, salt and water. Southern Italian bread is bursting with flavour, and hundreds of different varieties are baked to perfection on a daily basis. Stale bread is never wasted – it is used up in the form of breadcrumbs to top a baked dish or broken up into a bowl of vegetable soup. Durum wheat pasta is also absolutely fundamental to the eating habits of these regions. It has wonderful flavour and a firm texture, enabling it to be formed into many traditional shapes such as the ear-shaped orecchiette from Puglia, and strascinati, meaning 'stretched' or 'dragged' (referring to the way it is shaped), from Basilicata.

Couscous is part of the cultural legacy of the Arabic peoples who ruled Sicily for more than 150 years. These coarsely ground durum wheat grains are steamed and then eaten with vegetables, lamb or fish. The Arabs also brought rice to the shores of southern Italy, and the softer risotto rice forms the basis of savoury treats such as cheesy rice fritters, which are eaten as a lunchtime snack.

SWEET TREATS

There is a great tradition of making sweetmeats and desserts in southern Italy. Sicilians have a huge range of classic desserts and cakes to choose from, including cassata, cannoli, ice cream and refreshing jellies and sorbets. It is said that ice cream was first made in Sicily under the Arab domination using snow from the peak of Mount Etna, blended with honey and fruit. In Basilicata and Calabria, honey is used to sweeten local pastries. Sheep's milk ricotta is used as a creamy base for many different cakes and puddings, and almonds crop up frequently in pastries, biscuits (cookies) and cakes.

JASMINE FLOWERS AND ORANGE BLOSSOM

Sweet-smelling jasmine flowers are used to flavour and scent ice cream and jellies in many Sicilian dessert recipes. An extract of orange blossom is also used, and adds a strong, fragrant taste to a variety of Italian cakes and pastries.

DRINKS

Southern Italy has been producing full-bodied wine for over 4,000 years. In the 20th century, wine production languished, but is now beginning to pick up again, rivalling other regions such as Tuscany and Piedmont. In Calabria and Sicily, sweet dessert wines, known as vini da meditazione (wines for meditation), are made, including Marsala, Moscato, Zibbibo and Passito. They can be served at the end of the meal, or as an aperitif in the case of the drier varieties.

A vast range of local liqueurs are made in the south, including a bizarre drink made with the pulp of the prickly pear. Many of these, especially in Calabria and Basilicata, are home-made using just about any ingredients from basil leaves to chilli pepper to create powerful alcoholic drinks.

To cool and refresh during the hot summer days, locals in the south of Italy drink almond milk blended with sugar and water. In some places it is possible to buy this in cartons, or as a concentrate called orzata, which needs to be diluted before drinking.

AMARO

This dark brown, syrupy drink is sometimes consumed as a 'digestif' at the end of a large meal. It is made with a variety of unknown ingredients together with local herbs and tastes slightly medicinal. The name means 'bitter', which indeed describes it well.

ORECCHIETTE

To make orecchiette the traditional way, precise measurements are seldom used; the old guideline is to use roughly one handful of flour per person, but obviously this depends on the size of your hands.

MAKES 400G/14OZ (ABOUT 4 SERVINGS)

about 400g/14oz hard durum wheat flour
tepid water

1 Set aside a handful of flour for dusting, then mound the rest of the flour on to the work surface. Make a hollow in the centre of the mound. Add tepid water to the hollow. Using your hands, gradually mix the water with the surrounding flour to make a dough, adding more flour from the reserved quantity, if needed. The dough is ready for kneading when a thumb, inserted into it, comes away cleanly. Knead for 10 minutes, then form into a ball.

2 Squash the ball of dough on one side until it forms a point, applying your body's weight while rolling it. Continue rolling the point until it forms a long tubular shape. Roll this until a long string of dough, the thickness of your little finger, stretches out from the side of the ball, an arm's length long.

3 Using a non-serrated knife, cut the length into sections the size of a finger joint from tip to knuckle. With the knife blade at an angle of about 30 degrees, press down on the dough while pulling it backwards. This thins the dough and rolls it around the knife to form an oval. Invert it to look like an ear. Shape the remaining dough in the same way.

4 Place the orecchiette on a clean, floured cloth and leave to dry slightly before cooking. Alternatively, fully dry them and store in sealed jars for up to 1 year.

SOUPS AND ANTIPASTI
ZUPPE, MINESTRE E ANTIPASTI

In the southern regions of Italy, as elsewhere in the country, the traditional meal is made up of many different courses. The more special the occasion, such as a wedding, the more courses there should be in order to uphold the family honour! Antipasti are usually made with either vegetables, fish, cured meat, fresh meat or cheese, and often have bread involved as a vessel for the other ingredients and flavours; either as a slice to carry the other items or as breadcrumbs to surround and absorb the flavours. The antipasto always needs to be small, so as to leave plenty of room for the courses to come, but often there is such a huge selection available, especially in those regions where fresh fish often features as part of this course, that it is difficult not to gorge oneself on this delightful introduction to the rest of the meal.

THRIFTY SOUPS AND
DEEP-FRIED FRITTERS

In the poorer, more remote and isolated areas of the south, such as parts of Basilicata, a pot of soup is considered a good way to use up lots of different bits and pieces of vegetables and scraps of meat. This is then thickened and enriched with some stale bread and a good glug of rich green olive oil. There is one soup, from the city of Campobasso, that is made up of only three very cheap ingredients: salted water, stale bread and crumbled dried red chilli peppers. However, on the whole, soup tends to be quite rare in these regions, as the concept of warming bowls of soup seems superfluous in regions where the weather is mostly hot and dry.

Long southern meals tend to begin with a wide selection of antipasti, many of which are fried. However, in the coastal area near Bari, in Puglia, there is a tradition of eating raw seafood of all kinds, and locals consider this to be the most delicious antipasto option.

Dried, hot red chillies appear in the food of Calabria and Basilicata, less so in Puglia and Sicily, but nevertheless it is worth bearing in mind that dishes can be spicy even if they might look fairly innocuous.

The ubiquitous arancini and caponata are almost always part of an antipasto in Sicily. Arancini, little balls of cooked risotto rice mixed with all sorts of delicious ingredients, rolled in breadcrumbs and fried until golden and crisp, can be served at the beginning of a meal or as a snack at any time of the day. If they are part of an antipasto they tend to be small and elegant. Caponata is one of the island's best-loved aubergine (eggplant) recipes and has many variations. One particular favourite is the Caponata del Gattopardo, containing crunchy almonds, buried among the soft, oily aubergine cubes.

BREAD SOUP WITH POTATOES AND ROCKET
PANCOTTO CON RUCOLA E PATATE

This recipe is typical of La Cucina Povera; making something tasty out of practically nothing at all. Pancotto means 'cooked bread' and dishes with this title always have bread added for bulk, texture and flavour. There are many different versions of this dish in Italy, all of which arose from the need to feed the family in times of hardship.

1 Fill a large pan with cold water and add salt to taste. Peel the potatoes and slice them thickly. Immediately add them to the water and bring it to the boil.

2 Lower the heat and simmer the potatoes for 7 minutes.

3 Add the rocket and continue to cook until the potato slices are tender and have begun to disintegrate.

4 Add the bread, without breaking it up or removing the crusts, and mix thoroughly.

5 In a separate frying pan, heat the oil with the garlic and chilli. Cook for 2–3 minutes, to flavour the oil.

6 Pour the soup into a large heated bowl. Pour over the hot oil, holding back the chilli and garlic, and stir to mix. Discard the chilli and garlic. Serve immediately.

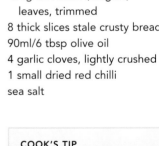

SERVES 4

500g/1¼lb potatoes
450g/1lb rocket (arugula)
    leaves, trimmed
8 thick slices stale crusty bread
90ml/6 tbsp olive oil
4 garlic cloves, lightly crushed
1 small dried red chilli
sea salt

COOK'S TIP

When flavouring the oil, do not let the garlic burn or the oil will taste bitter. Lift out the chilli and garlic as soon as you can smell the garlic strongly.

PER PORTION Energy 391kcal/1639kJ; Protein 9.8g; Carbohydrate 48.6g, of which sugars 4.7g; Fat 18.8g, of which saturates 2.8g; Cholesterol 0mg; Calcium 258mg; Fibre 4.4g; Sodium 452mg.

1 Savoy cabbage
2.5 litres/4½ pints/10 cups best
  beef stock
115g/4oz/1 cup freshly grated
  Pecorino cheese
8 thin slices toasted ciabatta
sea salt

COOK'S TIP

Make the beef stock with
marrow bones for the best
flavour, and spread the cooked
marrow from the bones over
the toasted ciabatta.

PER PORTION Energy 448kcal/1888kJ; Protein 24g;
Carbohydrate 60.8g, of which sugars 11.7g;
Fat 13.7g, of which saturates 6.5g; Cholesterol 29mg;
Calcium 552mg; Fibre 6g; Sodium 864mg.

GREEN CABBAGE SOUP
MINESTRA DI CAVOLO VERDE

This Calabrian recipe proves that as long as you use top quality ingredients – in this
case, first-class beef stock and crisp, flavoursome cabbage – you can transform a
basic dish into something special. The Pecorino is intrinsic to the flavour of this dish.
Make sure it is hard and very mature, and add a generous sprinkling to each portion.

1 Trim the cabbage, remove the core and all
the hard spines. Discard any really hard leaves,
shred the remaining cabbage very finely and
put it in a large pan. Pour over cold salted
water to cover. Bring to the boil and cook for
5 minutes, then drain and set aside.

2 Pour the stock into the clean pan and bring
it to the boil. Toss in the cabbage and cook it
again for 10 minutes.

3 Spoon into a large bowl and serve. Offer the
cheese and toasted ciabatta separately.

225g/8oz/1¼ cups dried broad (fava) beans
400g/14oz potatoes
about 2 large handfuls greens, such as cabbage or kale (optional)
100ml/3½fl oz/scant ½ cup extra virgin olive oil
sea salt

COOK'S TIP

Local cooks add a handful of wild greens picked fresh from the field. Bought greens such as spinach or kale are a good substitute, or you could leave them out altogether.

BROAD BEAN PURÉE
MACCU DI FAVE

'Fave' is the Italian name for the broad bean, but in Puglia, where this recipe comes from, the word is also used to describe this dense, oily mash based on broad beans and potatoes. Along with orecchiette, the ear-shaped pasta peculiar to the region, fave is a staple food. It is usually eaten as a first main course (primo piatto), as an alternative to pasta or risotto. Traditionally, it is topped with boiled bitter greens, creating a wonderful combination of textures and flavours.

1 Put the beans in a large pan or flameproof earthenware pot and cover generously with cold water. Bring to the boil, lower the heat and simmer gently for 2 hours.

2 Meanwhile, peel the potatoes, cut them into 2.5cm/1in slices and put them in a bowl of cold water. Leave to soak until the beans are ready.

3 After 2 hours, the pan of beans will have developed a foamy scum. Skim this off, then pour away most of the water by tilting the pan carefully over the sink.

4 Drain the potato slices and spread them over the semi-drained beans, then top up to the level of the potatoes with fresh water. Add a pinch of salt and return the pan to the heat for a further 30–40 minutes.

5 Meanwhile, if you intend topping the soup with greens, boil them in salted water for 10–20 minutes until tender.

6 Adjust the seasoning to taste, and then serve the soup in heated shallow bowls, with a generous swirl of olive oil on top of each portion and a topping of greens, if used.

PER PORTION Energy 314kcal/1317kJ; Protein 11.3g; Carbohydrate 32.7g, of which sugars 2.2g; Fat 16.3g, of which saturates 2.3g; Cholesterol 0mg; Calcium 50mg; Fibre 7.9g; Sodium 17mg.

WHITE BROAD BEAN SOUP
MINESTRA DI FAVE BIANCHE

Purity of ingredients and utter simplicity sum up this nourishing winter recipe.
In Puglia, where it originated, cooked rice or pastina (tiny pasta for soups) is often
added to a finished soup to make it more sustaining. This dish is similar to the
highly traditional, thick broad bean purée Maccu di Fave, which is eaten with a
topping of green oil and boiled bitter greens. This soup, however, is topped with
olive oil and a delicate sprinkling of freshly chopped chives.

1 Put the dried white broad beans in a large, heavy pan and pour over the water. Cover the pan and leave the beans to soak for at least 24 hours.

2 Transfer the pan with the beans and soaking liquid to the hob and bring to the boil.

3 Lower the heat. Simmer for 45–55 minutes, stirring frequently. Add more water if the purée appears to be drying out too much.

4 When the beans have disintegrated and are smooth and creamy, season with salt. Stir in the oil and sprinkle with chives and black pepper.

SERVES 4

500g/1¼lb/3 cups dried white
  broad (fava) beans (see Variation)
2 litres/3½ pints/8 cups water
90ml/6 tbsp olive oil
sea salt and ground black pepper
chives, finely chopped, to garnish

VARIATION

Dried white broad (fava) beans
are characteristic of the Puglia
region famed for this dish,
but dried butter beans or
dried green broad beans can
be used instead.

PER PORTION Energy 481kcal/2026kJ; Protein 27.6g;
Carbohydrate 55.1g, of which sugars 3.1g; Fat 18.2g,
of which saturates 2.6g; Cholesterol 0mg;
Calcium 125mg; Fibre 19.6g; Sodium 23mg.

AUBERGINE SKIN SALAD
INSALATA DI BUCCE DI MELANZANE

Thrifty Calabresi cooks make salads out of everything edible. Aubergines are often peeled when they are added to pasta sauces and casseroles, so this is a really canny way of using them up. The dish makes a lovely antipasto, gutsy and quite filling. It is delicious with salami or soppressata, or robust, aged Pecorino cheese.

1 Bring a large pan of salted water to the boil, add the aubergine skins and cook over a medium heat for 8 minutes.

2 Drain the aubergine skins and cut them into neat strips, no more than 2cm/¾in wide.

3 Put the warm strips in a salad bowl and stir in the oil to coat. Add the vinegar in the same way, and then add the garlic and herbs. Season with salt and pepper and toss well to mix. Leave to stand for 5 minutes before serving with crusty bread.

SERVES 4 TO 6

450g/1lb aubergine (eggplant) skins
135ml/9 tbsp olive oil
30ml/2 tbsp red wine vinegar
3 garlic cloves, chopped
8 fresh mint leaves, chopped
7.5ml/1½ tsp dried oregano
sea salt and ground black pepper
crusty bread, to serve

PER PORTION Energy 172kcal/708kJ; Protein 2.5g; Carbohydrate 2g, of which sugars 1.2g; Fat 17.1g, of which saturates 2.4g; Cholesterol 0mg; Calcium 129mg; Fibre 1.8g; Sodium 105mg.

SERVES 4

60ml/4 tbsp olive oil
3 large, strong-tasting onions,
   very thinly sliced
15ml/1 tbsp chopped fresh mint
115g/4oz/¾ cup salted capers,
   rinsed and chopped
sea salt
2–3 dried chillies, finely crushed

PER PORTION Energy 165kcal/681kJ; Protein 2.3g;
Carbohydrate 14.3g, of which sugars 10.2g;
Fat 11.4g, of which saturates 1.6g; Cholesterol 0mg;
Calcium 49mg; Fibre 2.6g; Sodium 497mg.

FRIED ONIONS WITH CAPERS AND CHILLI
CIPOLLE FRITTE CON CAPPERI

The flavours in this dish assault the senses and tingle the tastebuds. The recipe comes from the Basilicata region, where even the bread has a distinctive potency, though it is neither peppery nor particularly salty. This combination of onions, capers and chilli is perfect served as part of an antipasto with strong Italian cheese.

1 Pour the olive oil into a frying pan and heat slowly over a low heat.

2 Add the finely sliced onions and fry them gently for about 5 minutes until softened, but not coloured.

3 Raise the heat and stir the onions constantly for about 3 minutes until lightly browned.

4 Remove the pan from the heat. Stir in the mint and capers. Season with salt and stir in crushed dried chillies to taste. Cool before serving.

SICILIAN RICE FRITTERS
ARANCINI DI RISO

These delicious rice balls are on sale at every café in Sicily, and are eaten as a quick snack at any time of day. Few dishes say as much about the various nationalities who have contributed to the island over the centuries: the rice came from the Arabs; the cheese (traditionally a mild cheese called canestrato fresco but here replaced with mozzarella) was contributed by the Greeks; the ragù derives from the French ragoût and the tomato dipping sauce came from the Spanish. Arancini di riso are the pride of every rotisserie or Tavola Calda, although you'll seldom find them on restaurant menus.

1 Pour the stock into a pan and heat to simmering point. Keep it simmering while you cook the risotto.

2 Melt half the butter in a large heavy pan and add the onion. Cook over a very low heat for about 10 minutes, until the onion is soft but not coloured.

3 Stir the rice into the onion mixture and toast the grains thoroughly on all sides, so that they are opaque but not coloured. Add a ladleful of hot stock and stir it in until it has been absorbed.

4 Add a further two ladlefuls of hot stock and stir constantly so that the rice absorbs the liquid and all its flavour. Continue in this fashion, adding more stock only when the spoon draws a clear wake behind it as you draw it through the cooking rice.

5 After about 20 minutes, when the rice is soft and creamy, take the pan off the heat and stir in the cheese and the rest of the butter. Adjust the seasoning to taste and set aside to cool.

6 Put the cold risotto in a large bowl. Melt the butter in a small pan and sauté the mushrooms lightly. Add them to the risotto, with the peas, mozzarella and prosciutto.

7 Have the flour, beaten eggs and breadcrumbs ready in separate shallow bowls.

8 Shape the rice mixture into balls, about the size of tangerines. If you want to fill them with ragù, make an indentation in each ball, spoon in 5ml/1 tsp of ragù, then reshape the rice so that the ragù is enclosed.

9 Roll the balls in the flour, then the eggs and finally the dried breadcrumbs.

10 Heat the oil in a large pan to 180°C/350°F, or until a cube of bread, dropped into the oil, browns in about 45 seconds. Fry the balls, in batches, for 6–8 minutes until golden. Drain on kitchen paper. Serve hot, with the tomato sauce for dipping, if you like.

MAKES ABOUT 20

FOR THE RISOTTO

1.5 litres/2½ pints/6 cups hot chicken, meat or vegetable stock
75g/3oz/6 tbsp unsalted butter
1 onion, finely chopped
600g/1lb 6oz/2½ cups risotto rice, preferably Vialone Nano
90–105ml/6–7 tbsp freshly grated Parmesan cheese

FOR THE FRITTERS

15g/½ oz/1 tbsp butter
50g/2oz/½ cup mushrooms, sliced
100g/3½oz/scant 1 cup cooked peas
80g/3¼oz mozzarella cheese, diced
50g/2oz prosciutto, finely chopped
45ml/3 tbsp plain (all-purpose) flour
3 eggs, beaten
90ml/6 tbsp white dried breadcrumbs
1 quantity Ragù (see p17; optional)
sea salt and ground black pepper
sunflower oil, for deep-frying
1 quantity tomato sauce (see Cook's Tip), for dipping (optional)

COOK'S TIP

To make a tomato sauce for dipping, heat 60ml/4 tbsp olive oil in a pan and gently fry 1 finely chopped onion, 1 finely chopped celery stick and 1 finely chopped carrot for about 10 minutes until soft. Do not let the onion brown. Add 500g/1¼lb fresh or canned tomatoes, cover and simmer for 30 minutes, stirring regularly. Season to taste.

500g/1¼lb/8 cups mushrooms
2 eggs, beaten
3 garlic cloves, very finely chopped
45ml/3 tbsp chopped fresh parsley
45ml/3 tbsp grated Pecorino cheese
45ml/3 tbsp fresh white
  breadcrumbs
sunflower oil, for deep-frying
sea salt and ground black pepper

SICILIAN MUSHROOM FRITTERS
POLPETTE DI FUNGHI

These little fritters make a wonderful canapé or antipasto dish. They taste especially delicious when handed around with a garlicky dip, possibly with a yogurt or sour cream base, or with traditional l'arrabiata. Whichever type of mushrooms you choose, make sure they have a soft texture.

1 Fill the base of a steamer (or a pan fitted with a steamer basket) with water and bring to the boil. Put the mushrooms in the steamer or steamer basket and steam until just cooked.

2 Squeeze the mushrooms to remove some of the moisture and then chop them very finely in a food processor or with a heavy-bladed knife.

3 Put the chopped mushrooms in a bowl and add the eggs, garlic, parsley, cheese and breadcrumbs. Season with salt and plenty of ground black pepper. Mix well.

4 Shape the mixture into 24 balls and flatten these to make round fritters.

5 Heat the oil for deep-frying to 180°C/350°F or until a small piece of bread, dropped into the oil, browns in about 45 seconds. Fry the fritters, in batches if necessary, for 2–3 minutes until they rise to the surface and are crisp and golden.

6 Remove with a slotted spoon, drain on kitchen paper and keep hot while cooking successive batches. When all the fritters are cooked, serve them immediately.

PER FRITTER Energy 66kcal/274kJ; Protein 1.9g; Carbohydrate 1.6g, of which sugars 0.1g; Fat 5.9g, of which saturates 1.1g; Cholesterol 18mg; Calcium 33mg; Fibre 0.4g; Sodium 42mg.

ANCHOVY FRITTERS
CRISPEDDI A LICI

To make the batter for this recipe in the traditional Calabrian style, you need a bavanu, a classic terracotta bowl with a glazed lining. Whichever bowl you use, make sure it is a large one and be sure to use only your hands to beat the batter in order to make it really tacky and light. The fritters make a lovely tasty snack, especially when served with plenty of dry white wine.

1 Put the flour into a bowl and make a well in the centre.

2 Pour the water into a cup and crumble in the yeast. Pour the mixture into the well in the flour. Using your hands, mix the water into the flour, adding more water if required to make a sticky, stringy mass. Be careful not to add too much liquid.

3 Knead the batter by beating with your hands in a circular motion for about 30 minutes. Beat in the salt. Cover the bowl with a cloth and leave the batter to rise at warm room temperature for 3–4 hours. Meanwhile, roughly chop the anchovies.

4 Heat the oil in a large pan to 180°C/350°F or until a small cube of bread, dropped into the oil, browns in about 45 seconds.

5 Using your hand, scoop up about a tablespoon of batter and stretch it slightly with your fingers. Tuck a piece of anchovy inside and drop the dough into the hot oil. Add more pieces of dough in the same way but do not overcrowd the pan.

6 Fry the fritters, in batches, for 4–6 minutes until they rise to the surface of the oil and turn crisp and golden, then lift them out with a slotted spoon and drain on kitchen paper. Serve at once – the hotter the better.

SERVES 12

lkg/2¼lb/9 cups plain
  (all-purpose) flour
120ml/4fl oz/½ cup hand-hot water
50g/2oz fresh (compressed) yeast
1.5ml/¼ tsp salt
300g/11oz salted anchovies,
  rinsed, boned and dried
sunflower oil or light olive oil,
  for deep-frying

COOK'S TIP

Rinse the anchovies very well, to remove the surplus salt, and take care to remove the bones. Dry them with kitchen paper before chopping.

PER PORTION Energy 416kcal/1753kJ; Protein 14.5g; Carbohydrate 64.9g, of which sugars 1.3g; Fat 12.7g, of which saturates 2.1g; Cholesterol 0mg; Calcium 141mg; Fibre 2.6g; Sodium 34.6mg.

FRIED PRIEST STRANGLERS
STRANGOLAPRETI FRITTI

There are many explanations for how this recipe from Basilicata got its name; almost as many as there are versions of the dish itself. It can be a pasta, a dessert or, as here, a platter of tiny fritters to be served as an antipasto. The story (and the recipe) varies depending upon where you are in Italy. One of the best tales concerns a cook who took revenge upon a notoriously greedy priest by preparing this speciality in his honour. The fritters were so tasty and the priest so greedy that the cook knew he would stuff himself with them until he choked. Which he did.

1 Put the flour on to a clean work surface and make a hollow in the centre.

2 Break the eggs into the hollow and add the salt and the lemon rind. Mix the eggs, gradually incorporating the surrounding flour to make a dough. Knead the dough energetically; it should be dense and tight. Wrap it in clear film (plastic wrap) and leave to rest for 10 minutes.

3 Unwrap the dough and divide it into 10–12 pieces. Shape each piece into a sausage and roll on the work surface to lengthen and thin the dough until the each piece is the same size and shape as grissini (breadsticks). Cut each thin roll into 2.5cm/1in lengths.

4 Press each piece of dough against the back of a curved cheese grater so that it becomes concave on one side and marked with the grooves of the grater on the other. Lay the shaped pieces on a lightly floured work surface or clean dish towel.

5 Heat the oil for deep-frying to 180°C/350°F or until a small piece of bread, dropped into the oil, browns in about 45 seconds. Fry the shapes, in batches, for 2–4 minutes or until the fritters have risen to the surface of the oil and are puffy and golden.

6 Drain on kitchen paper and keep hot while cooking successive batches. Serve immediately.

SERVES 6 TO 10

300g/11oz/2¾ cups fine pasta flour
   or fine-milled plain (all-purpose)
   white flour
3 eggs
1.5ml/¼ tsp salt
grated rind of I lemon
olive oil, for deep-frying

PER PORTION Energy 194kcal/811kJ; Protein 4.7g; Carbohydrate 23.3g, of which sugars 0.5g; Fat 9.8g, of which saturates 1.6g; Cholesterol 57mg; Calcium 51mg; Fibre 0.9g; Sodium 22mg.

SERVES 4 TO 6

400g/14oz/3½ cups strong white
   bread flour
15g/½oz fresh (compressed) yeast
20 marinated green olives, pitted
7 or 8 salted anchovies, rinsed,
   boned and chopped
175ml/6fl oz/¾ cup olive oil
ground black pepper

PER PORTION Energy 482kcal/2013kJ; Protein 7.8g;
Carbohydrate 51.8g, of which sugars 1g; Fat 28.4g,
of which saturates 3.9g; Cholesterol 0mg;
Calcium 117mg; Fibre 2.4g; Sodium 456mg.

OLIVE AND ANCHOVY BREAD
SFOGLIATA CON OLIVE E ACCIUGHE

This is a light loaf from Puglia with lots of flavour and a lovely texture. To prepare the dough the traditional way you really need on-the-spot training from a local baker, but this recipe is a good start. Serve the bread as part of an antipasto course, with a richly dressed tomato salad and some chilli-spiked salami and sliced prosciutto, or with a selection of seafood dressed with olive oil, chilli and garlic. Serve warm or cold.

1 Pile the flour on a clean work surface and plunge your fist in the top to make a hollow all the way through.

2 Mash the yeast in a small bowl with just enough water to make a thick liquid. Pour this into the hollow, add about one-third of the olive oil and knead together very thoroughly with your hands, making a dough that is as pliable and elastic as possible.

3 When the dough comes away easily from your hands, divide it into smallish lumps and roll each lump out to a disc that is about the size of a side plate. Place each dough disc on a separate plate, cover with cloths and leave in a warm place to rise until doubled in bulk. This should take about 30 minutes.

4 Preheat the oven to 180°C/350°F/Gas 4. Brush an oval baking dish, about 18cm in length, with some of the remaining oil. Knock back (punch down) the discs and flatten them. Scatter each disc with a few olives, a few pieces of anchovy and a little olive oil.

5 Roll a disc up loosely to make a tube shape about 2.5–3cm/1–1¼in thick, then stand it on end and push it down from the top to squash it slightly. Repeat for the remaining discs.

6 Stand all the squashed tubes side by side in the baking dish. Push them up tight against one another to make one big loaf. Brush the surface with oil and bake for 40 minutes, until the loaf is well risen and is golden brown. Remove from the dish and cool on a wire rack.

SICILIAN ONION AND TOMATO PIZZA
SFINCIUNI

This dish has ancient roots and is sometimes called schiavazza or rianata. One of the most famous versions was prepared by the nuns of the San Vito and Sfinciuni di Santu is still famous in the city of Palermo in Sicily. Unlike the thin and crispy pizzas usually associated with Italy, this simple Sicilian classic is sometimes half as deep as it is wide, and it has a soft and spongy texture.

1 Spoon 75ml/5 tbsp hand-hot water into a small bowl. Crumble in the yeast, stir and set aside. Pile the flour on a clean work surface and make a hollow in the centre with your fist. Add 2.5ml/½ tsp each of salt and pepper to the hollow, then spoon in one-third of the grated cheese.

2 Pour 45ml/3 tbsp of the olive oil into a small pan and add the lemon juice. Warm until it is hand-hot, pour into the hollow, then add the yeast mixture. Stir, gradually incorporating the surrounding flour. Add more warm water if needed and knead to a smooth, elastic dough. Knead the dough energetically for 10–15 minutes more, then roll it into a ball and place it in a large bowl. Cut a cross in the top of the ball. Cover with a cloth or clear film (plastic wrap). Leave to rise for 2 hours in a warm place.

3 Meanwhile, put the tomatoes in a bowl of boiling water for 1–2 minutes. Remove with a slotted spoon and peel. Halve them, remove the seeds and chop the flesh.

4 Heat 60ml/4 tbsp of the olive oil in a pan and fry the onion for 4–5 minutes, until transparent. Add the tomatoes. Season. Simmer for 1 hour, stirring occasionally.

5 Grease an 18cm/7in square cake tin (pan) at least 10cm/4in deep (see Cook's Tip) with olive oil. Knock back (punch down) the risen dough, then knead for 10 minutes. Pat it out to the shape of the prepared cake tin. Cover and leave to rise again in a warm place for 30 minutes.

6 Meanwhile, add the parsley, half the anchovies and half the remaining cheese to the tomato sauce. Mix well.

7 Preheat the oven to 200°C/400°F/Gas 6. When the dough has risen again, press a clean finger deeply into the dough at 5cm/2in intervals. Reserving a little, fill the hollows with the sauce, spreading some over the surface.

8 Bake for 25 minutes. Meanwhile, heat 45ml/3 tbsp of the remaining oil in a small frying pan and fry the breadcrumbs until crisp. Take the pizza out of the oven, spread the surface with the reserved tomato sauce, top with the remaining anchovies and cheese, then scatter the breadcrumbs over. Add a generous drizzle of olive oil and return to the oven for 10 minutes more. Serve.

PER PIZZA Energy 3119kcal/12997kJ; Protein 74.2g; Carbohydrate 236g, of which sugars 24.3g; Fat 215.3g, of which saturates 40.9g; Cholesterol 75mg; Calcium 1585mg; Fibre 16.8g; Sodium 2975mg.

MAKES ONE 18CM/7IN PIZZA

35g/1¼oz fresh (compressed) yeast
250g/9oz//2⅓ cups plain (all-purpose) flour, plus extra for dusting and kneading
75g/3oz/¾ cup freshly grated Pecorino or Caciocavallo cheese
250ml/8fl oz/1 cup olive oil
juice of I lemon
500g/1¼lb ripe tomatoes
1 small onion, thinly sliced
50g/2oz/1 cup fresh parsley, finely chopped
5 large salted anchovies, rinsed, boned and chopped
15–30ml/1–2 tbsp coarse white breadcrumbs
sea salt and ground black pepper

VARIATION

In Sicily, sausage meat (bulk sausage) is sometimes spread over the dough with a little tomato sauce. It is then topped with a second layer of dough before being baked.

COOK'S TIP

The easiest way to make this pizza is to use a spring-release tin (pan) or a loose-bottomed cake tin. If you do not have one of these, use a regular cake tin, but line it with a wide strip of baking parchment. The parchment strip should be long enough to extend beyond the rim of the tin on both sides, giving you 'handles' for lifting out the pizza.

PASTA AND RICE
PASTA E RISO

Good-quality dried pasta is enormously popular in these regions, perhaps more so than anywhere else in the country. The relatively simple idea of a dish of pasta tossed with a sauce, known collectively as pastasciutta, is brought to life in southern Italy. Dried durum wheat pasta (which comes in a multitude of shapes) is boiled in lots of salted water, drained when al dente, then dressed with one of countless sauces containing anything from fish and shellfish to vegetables, but usually very little meat other than the odd strip of pancetta to add flavour. Rice is used to some extent in Sicily, but plays a very minor role anywhere else in these regions and risotto is a rarity. Polenta and gnocchi simply do not feature here; they are associated with the freezing cold, foggy days and nights of Italy's northern regions, such as Lombardy, the Veneto and Piedmont, which feel a million miles away from the sun-baked south.

ORECCHIETTE, SPAGHETTI AND SPICY SAUCES

The southern regions have always been famously associated with dried pasta, not only for their love and appreciation of dried pasta dishes, but for their long tradition of growing some of the world's finest durum wheat, which is needed to make the best pasta. All over these southern regions, a tradition of sowing, reaping, milling and mixing goes back for centuries. Nowadays, demand for dried durum wheat pasta far outstrips the local production, so a great deal of the grain is imported, but a handful of the small, artisanal pasta factories still do exist and they continue to produce pasta of very high quality which is much sought after by local connoisseurs.

This kind of pasta is made by mixing durum wheat flour with water. The resulting dough is shaped and dried into over 650 shapes. Each and every region has its special favourite shapes: in Sicily, they adore anelli, the ring-shaped pasta that is used in all sorts of local recipes; in Puglia, they love to hand-make 'little ears' or orecchiette. Making this kind of hand-made dough produces very dense, heavy shapes that are mixed with specific local sauces to make extremely sustaining pasta dishes. The finer, smoother, golden-coloured pasta, such as penne, bucatini or maccheroni, is made under factory conditions, where the mixing, cutting and drying processes are much more sophisticated. Whatever the shape, there is no place here for the egg and flour version of pasta, known as La Sfoglia, that gets turned into pasta dishes such as Tagliatelle al Ragù or Lasagna in the northern regions. They may both be known as pasta, but the name really is where the similarity between the pasta of the north and that of the south ends.

SPAGHETTI WITH CAPERS AND YELLOW PEPPER
SPAGHETTI ALLA SIRACUSANA

This simple recipe from the ancient and atmospheric city of Siracusa makes for a delicious and very attractive pasta dish. Only the sweetest, juiciest yellow peppers, such as those that grow in rich profusion all over Sicily, should be used to achieve the right intensity of sweet, slightly peppery flavour.

1 Roast the yellow pepper over a naked flame or under a hot grill (broiler), turning it frequently until the skin blisters and is blackened all over.

2 Put the pepper in a bowl, cover the bowl with clear film (plastic wrap) and set aside.

3 Heat the oil in a pan and add the garlic. As soon as the garlic turns brown, lift it out with a slotted spoon and discard.

4 Add the anchovies to the flavoured oil and cook for 2–3 minutes, mashing them with a wooden spoon until they form a smooth brown purée.

5 Pull off the skin from the roasted pepper, removing any stubborn pieces with a sharp knife. Cut the pepper in half, remove the seeds and membranes and chop the flesh into small squares. Add these to the anchovy mixture with the aubergine cubes and tomatoes.

6 Stir in the olives, basil and capers, with a little salt, if needed, to taste. Cover the pan and simmer until the vegetables are soft.

7 Bring a large pan of salted water to the boil. Add the spaghetti and cook for 12–14 minutes until just tender. Drain the pasta and put it into a warmed bowl. Pour over the sauce, toss to mix, and serve.

SERVES 4

1 large yellow (bell) pepper
120ml/4fl oz/½ cup olive oil
2 garlic cloves, lightly crushed
3 large, salted anchovies, washed, dried and boned
1 large aubergine (eggplant), peeled and cubed
275g/10oz ripe tomatoes, peeled, seeded and cut in quarters
4 black olives, pitted and chopped
4 green olives, pitted and chopped
8 fresh basil leaves, torn into shreds
15–20ml/3–4 tsp salted capers, rinsed, dried and chopped
400g/14oz dried spaghetti
sea salt (optional)

PER PORTION Energy 569kcal/2394kJ; Protein 14.4g; Carbohydrate 80.1g, of which sugars 9.1g; Fat 23.5g, of which saturates 3.2g; Cholesterol 0mg; Calcium 56mg; Fibre 5.6g; Sodium 384mg.

SERVES 4

60ml/4 tbsp olive oil

3 garlic cloves, chopped

225g/8oz fresh, ripe tomatoes,
 quartered and seeded

10 fresh basil leaves, torn into shreds

115g/4oz/1 cup coarse dried
 breadcrumbs

30–45ml/2–3 tbsp grated Pecorino
 or Parmesan cheese

60ml/4 tbsp chopped fresh
 flat leaf parsley

450g/1lb/4 cups anelli or other
 pasta shapes

sea salt

ANELLI WITH BREADCRUMBS
ANELLI AMMUDDICATI

In southern Italy, especially Sicily and Calabria, fine, stale breadcrumbs are often used instead of grated cheese on pasta. This is either because there is simply no cheese available, or a hangover from the days when there was no money for cheese. Sometimes the breadcrumbs are fried for extra texture.

1 Pour the oil into a large pan and add the garlic. Fry for 2–3 minutes, until the garlic is transparent, then add the tomatoes and basil. Stir in salt to taste, then cover and simmer the mixture for 20 minutes on a medium heat. Add water if the sauce becomes too thick.

2 Bring a large pan of salted water to the boil. Meanwhile, put the breadcrumbs in a small bowl and add the cheese and parsley.

3 When the tomato sauce is almost ready, add the pasta to the boiling water. Bring it back to the boil, then cook the pasta for 12–14 minutes, until just tender, then drain and return to the pan.

4 Pour over the tomato sauce and toss well. Divide the mixture among four bowls, sprinkle each portion generously with the breadcrumb mixture and serve at once.

COOK'S TIPS

• Instead of anelli, you could use maccheroncelli (a thin tubular shape, slightly thinner than a pencil) or pennette (short, thin penne).

• Use sweet, sun-ripened tomatoes so the sauce has no trace of the sour flavour that unripe tomatoes tend to impart.

PER PORTION Energy 650kcal/2748kJ; Protein 22g; Carbohydrate 107.7g, of which sugars 6.5g; Fat 17.6g, of which saturates 4.1g; Cholesterol 11mg; Calcium 230mg; Fibre 5.1g; Sodium 354mg.

HOME-MADE PASTA WITH CHICKPEAS
LAGANE E CECI

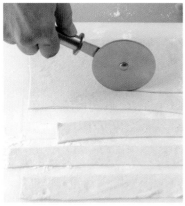

This is one of those very simple, yet tasty, dishes that was born out of the poverty that the people of Basilicata have endured throughout history. In this remote area, ingredients have always been extremely limited – what could not be cultivated or bred in the severe climate simply did not exist. Even today, unusual ingredients are hard to come by and local cooks continue to prepare the traditional dishes that have been handed down by previous generations.

1 Put the chickpeas in a large bowl and cover with plenty of cold water. Cover the bowl and leave the chickpeas to soak overnight.

2 Drain the chickpeas and put them in a large pan. Pour in cold water to cover, bring to the boil and boil hard over a high heat for 5 minutes.

3 Drain the chickpeas again, rinse them thoroughly and return them to the pan. Cover with fresh water. Bring to the boil, reduce the heat and simmer for about 2 hours over a low heat, or until the chickpeas are soft and tender. Top up the water as needed during the cooking time.

4 Once the chickpeas have been cooking for 2 hours, check the water levels, top up if necessary and cook for a further hour while you make the pasta.

5 Put the flour on to a clean work surface. Make a hollow in the centre and add a little salt. Pour about a quarter of the measured water into the hollow. Gradually incorporate the surrounding flour, adding more water as needed, to make a dough. Knead until smooth and elastic.

6 Roll the dough out on a floured surface to a very thin sheet. Using a pastry wheel, cut it into 2.5cm/1in strips. Leave these to dry for 15 minutes.

7 When the chickpeas have been cooking for 3 hours in total, drain any remaining liquid and season them with salt. Keep them warm.

8 Heat the oil in a pan and fry the garlic and onion gently for about 5 minutes, until the onion is soft and golden brown.

9 Bring a large pan of salted water to the boil. Add the pasta strips and cook for about 5 minutes or until tender.

10 Drain and transfer to a large warmed bowl. Add the chickpeas and the fried onion and garlic, toss everything together and serve. Garnish with a dried chilli, if you like.

SERVES 4

500g/1¼lb/3 cups dried chickpeas
500g/1¼lb/5 cups plain (all-purpose) white flour
500ml/18fl oz/generous 2 cups water
75ml/5 tbsp olive oil
2 garlic cloves, finely chopped
½ onion, sliced
sea salt
dried red chilli, to garnish (optional)

COOK'S TIPS

• Getting the pasta dough to the correct texture so that it can be rolled to a fine sheet takes time and considerable energy. The best way to learn is by observing an experienced cook; if this isn't possible, persevere until you develop the knack.
• A good way to dry the strips of pasta is to place a clean dish towel over the back of a kitchen chair, then carefully drape the pasta over this.

PER PORTION Energy 955kcal/4037kJ; Protein 38.6g; Carbohydrate 160.3g, of which sugars 6g; Fat 22.2g, of which saturates 2.8g; Cholesterol 0mg; Calcium 379mg; Fibre 17.5g; Sodium 53mg.

SERVES 4

150ml/¼ pint/⅔ cup olive oil
3 garlic cloves
4 whole dried red chillies
60ml/4 tbsp tomato purée (paste)
400g/14oz dried orecchiette

ORECCHIETTE WITH GARLIC AND CHILLI
ORECCHIETTE CON AGLIO E PEPERONCINO

All pasta shapes work well in this incredibly fiery pasta dish, but orecchiette are particularly suitable, since their blandness and chewy texture act as a perfect foil for the hot sauce. The region that created this recipe, Basilicata, is famous for its use of chilli (known locally as il diavolino or 'the little devil'), which locals eat in large quantities and intensity without any obvious ill-effects.

1 Bring a large pan of salted water to the boil.

2 Heat the oil in a different very large pan. Add the garlic and chillies and fry over low to medium heat for 3–4 minutes, until the garlic is soft and golden brown and the chillies are very shiny and swollen. Do not let either burn.

3 Scoop the garlic and chillies out of the oil with a slotted spoon.

4 Put the garlic and chillies in a food processor or blender and add the tomato purée. Process until smooth, then stir back into the oil remaining in the pan.

5 Add the pasta to the boiling water. Cook for 12–14 minutes until just tender, then drain. Transfer it into the pan containing the garlic and chilli mixture. Toss over the heat until the pasta is coated with the sauce, then serve.

COOK'S TIPS

• For a milder flavour, use fewer chillies.
• The garlic, chilli and tomato purée (paste) can be pounded together in a large mortar using a pestle and then the oil incorporated to achieve more or less the same effect as with a food processor.

PER PORTION Energy 577kcal/2424kJ; Protein 12.7g; Carbohydrate 76g, of which sugars 5.2g; Fat 26.8g, of which saturates 3.7g; Cholesterol 0mg; Calcium 32mg; Fibre 3.3g; Sodium 39mg.

ORECCHIETTE WITH CAULIFLOWER
ORECCHIETTE CON IL CAVOLFIORE

Orecchiette means 'little ears' and that's exactly what these dense, hard pasta shapes look like. Made from just flour and water, they require skill and patience to make by hand, as well as plenty of time and lots of effort, so many cooks prefer to simply buy a packet of dried orecchiette. This dish is from Puglia.

1 Place the lardons or pancetta in a frying pan. Heat gently until the fat runs, then cook without browning for about 10 minutes.

2 Meanwhile, bring a large pan of salted water to the boil. Add the cauliflower florets and cook them for 5–7 minutes.

3 Add the orecchiette to the pan, stir once and cook for 2–3 minutes, or until the pasta shapes rise to the surface of the water.

4 Drain the cauliflower and the orecchiette, and transfer the mixture into a warmed serving bowl.

5 Add the fried lardons or pancetta and the grated Pecorino cheese to the orecchiette and cauliflower mixture.

6 Add a generous grinding of black pepper, toss well to mix all of the ingredients together and serve immediately.

SERVES 4

115g/4oz bacon lardons or
  pancetta, cubed
1kg/2¼lb green cauliflower florets
400g/14oz fresh orecchiette
115g/4oz/1⅓ cups grated
  Pecorino cheese
sea salt and ground black pepper

VARIATIONS
. . . .
• You could use streaky (fatty) bacon instead of pancetta or lardons, if you like, but fry it until crisp before adding it to the pasta.
• You can also use dried orecchiette for this dish, but since the pasta takes longer to cook than the cauliflower, add the cauliflower towards the end of cooking.

PER PORTION Energy 636kcal/2680kJ; Protein 36.9g; Carbohydrate 81.6g, of which sugars 9.6g; Fat 20.2g, of which saturates 9g; Cholesterol 47mg; Calcium 424mg; Fibre 7.4g; Sodium 701mg.

PASTA WITH FRESH SARDINES
PASTA CON LE SARDE

The ingredient that gives this dish its unique aniseed flavour is wild fennel. It is not only used in the sauce, but also flavours the pasta, which is boiled in the water in which the fennel was cooked. Saffron and fresh sardines complete the palette of flavours, unique to this most Sicilian of pasta dishes.

1 Put the sultanas in a small bowl. Pour over warm water to cover and set aside for 15 minutes.

2 Put the saffron in a separate bowl and stir in 45ml/3 tbsp cold water.

3 Meanwhile, put the fennel in a large pan with the salt and the measured water. Bring to the boil, lower the heat and cover the pan. Simmer for 10 minutes.

4 Remove the fennel with a slotted spoon and put it in a seive (strainer) until cool enough to handle. Squeeze the fennel in your hands over a bowl to remove the moisture, then put it on to a board and chop it very finely. Set the pan with the cooking water aside.

5 Put the onion in a large pan and cover generously with water. Bring to the boil, then simmer over a medium heat for about 10 minutes or until the onion is soft.

6 Add half the olive oil, the saffron with its soaking water, and the pine nuts to the cooked onion. Drain the sultanas and stir them into the pan. Simmer, stirring frequently, for 10 minutes.

7 Stir in the chopped fennel and the prepared sardines. Cover the pan and cook over a very low heat, turning the fish frequently, for 4–5 minutes, until the sardines are cooked through.

8 Meanwhile, in a separate pan, cook the anchovies for 2–3 minutes in the remaining olive oil, mashing them into a smooth brown purée.

9 When the sardines are cooked, stir in the anchovy purée. Mix well and season to taste with salt and black pepper. Keep the mixture warm.

10 Return the pan used for cooking the fennel to the heat. Taste and add salt if necessary. Bring to the boil, add the pasta and stir. Cook fresh pasta for about 4 minutes; dried pasta for 12–14 minutes.

11 When the pasta is tender, drain it well, transfer it into a warmed bowl and pour over the sauce. Toss thoroughly and serve.

PER PORTION Energy 478kcal/2007kJ; Protein 20g; Carbohydrate 57.4g, of which sugars 9.1g; Fat 20.3g, of which saturates 3.1g; Cholesterol 0mg; Calcium 90mg; Fibre 3.4g; Sodium 226mg.

SERVES 4 TO 6

30ml/2 tbsp sultanas (golden raisins)
1 sachet saffron powder
150g/5oz wild fennel (leaves and stalks), washed and trimmed
10ml/2 tsp fine salt
2 litres/3½ pints/8 cups cold water
1 large onion, chopped
90ml/6 tbsp olive oil
25g/1oz/⅓ cup pine nuts
275g/10oz fresh or thawed frozen sardines, cleaned, boned and with heads removed
2 whole salted anchovies, boned and washed
400g/14oz fresh or dried bucatini, thick perciatelli or other pasta shapes
sea salt and ground black pepper

COOK'S TIP

If wild fennel proves hard to find, buy some leafy fennel bulbs. Cut off all the feathery leaves, then use the harder outer leaves and the stalks to make up the weight. This is a good way of using the parts of the vegetable that might otherwise be discarded, but which give excellent flavour to the dish.

VERMICELLI WITH SQUID INK
VERMICELLI AL NERO DI SEPPIE

Using really fresh squid is key here, as this will ensure the sweetest and most fragrant finished dish. The truly authentic recipe calls for strattu, an amazingly tasty sun-dried tomato paste, which is available in all good food shops and market stalls on the island of Sicily, but is less easy to find anywhere else. Good-quality concentrated tomato purée is the best substitute.

1 Rinse the squid thoroughly. Holding one firmly, grasp the tentacles at the base and pull the head and entrails away from the body. Cut off the tentacles from the head and set them aside. Discard the head with the hard 'beak' but retain the ink sac, which looks like a black vein. Peel the membrane from the body, then pull out and discard the 'quill'.

2 Cut the body of the squid into small cubes. Chop the tentacles finely. Repeat with the rest of the squid. Rinse and dry all the squid well.

3 Heat the olive oil over a medium heat in a large pan. Add the garlic cloves, fry until brown, then remove with a slotted spoon and discard.

4 Add the squid to the garlic-flavoured oil. Stir in the parsley and plenty of pepper. Cover and simmer the mixture for 45 minutes.

5 Pour over the white wine and add the strattu or tomato purée. Stir well and continue to simmer, uncovered, for 20 minutes.

6 Lower the heat, cover the pan again and cook for a further 30 minutes, adding a little hot water as and when needed to dilute the sauce.

7 About 15–17 minutes before serving, bring a large pan of salted water to the boil. Add the pasta, stir and cook for 10–12 minutes over a medium heat until just tender.

8 Meanwhile, add the ink sacs to the sauce and stir to mix.

9 Drain the pasta well and return it to the pan. Pour the sauce over and mix thoroughly. Cover and leave to stand for 5 minutes, then turn out on to a platter and serve at once.

SERVES 4 TO 6

whole fresh squid with ink sac (around 500g/1¼lb)
60ml/4 tbsp olive oil
2–3 whole garlic cloves, bruised
45ml/3 tbsp chopped fresh parsley
100ml/3½fl oz/scant ½ cup dry white wine
15ml/1 tbsp strattu or 45ml/3 tbsp concentrated tomato purée (paste)
400g/14oz vermicelli
sea salt and ground black pepper

COOK'S TIP

If you cannot find fresh, whole squid, use ready-to-use squid and buy the ink separately in a sachet or jar from a fishmonger or Italian food shop. Take care when handling the ink sacs, as squid ink stains clothing and turns fingernails black.

PER PORTION Energy 383kcal/1603kJ; Protein 18.9g; Carbohydrate 53.5g, of which sugars 0.3g; Fat 9.1g, of which saturates 1.4g; Cholesterol 188mg; Calcium 40mg; Fibre 0.3g; Sodium 100mg.

SERVES 4

500g/1¼lb live mussels or cooked
    mussels in their shells
350g/12oz dried maccheroncini
    or spaghetti
60ml/4 tbsp olive oil
2 garlic cloves, finely chopped
45ml/3 tbsp chopped fresh parsley
400g/14oz chopped and seeded
    ripe tomatoes, drained
sea salt and ground black pepper

PER PORTION Energy 452kcal/1910kJ; Protein 18.1g;
Carbohydrate 68.3g, of which sugars 6.3g; Fat 13.8g,
of which saturates 2g; Cholesterol 15mg;
Calcium 128mg; Fibre 4.2g; Sodium 95mg.

PASTA WITH MUSSELS
PASTA CON LE COZZE

This is one of the easiest ways to enjoy the delicious combination of pasta with shellfish. The recipe is a famous speciality of Campo Marino, a seaside resort on the Ionian coast in the province of Salento in Puglia. Mussels are extremely popular in the area, and the locals like to eat them raw with just a squeeze of lemon juice. In this recipe, they are flavoured almost as simply, with oil, garlic and parsley.

1 If using fresh mussels, check them and discard any that are not tightly closed, or that do not snap shut when tapped on the work surface. Scrub all the mussels carefully and rinse them thoroughly.

2 Place the cleaned mussels in a wide frying pan. Cover the pan and place over medium-high heat for 5–6 minutes, shaking the pan frequently, until the mussels have opened. Any mussels that have not opened after this time should be discarded.

3 Remove all the mussels from the open shells, wipe off any traces of sand or sediment, and set them aside. Discard the shells.

4 Bring a large pan of lightly salted water to the boil and add the dried pasta. Stir, return to the boil and cook for 12–14 minutes or until just tender.

5 Meanwhile, heat the oil in a large frying pan and add the garlic and parsley. Fry for 5 minutes, then add the tomatoes. Season, stir, and cook over a high heat for about 8 minutes. Stir in the mussels.

6 Drain the cooked pasta and add it to the pan containing the mussels and tomatoes.

7 Stir to coat the pasta in the sauce, then serve in warmed bowls.

PASTA WITH POTENZA RAGÙ
PASTA AL RAGÙ POTENTINO

Potenza, the regional capital of Basilicata, is famous for having the most extreme temperatures in Italy. When the weather is icy, a one-pot dish like this one is ideal. The sauce is cooked with a large piece of flattened pork or beef in it to impart a rich flavour. In Potenza, the pasta and the sauce would be served as a substantial, nourishing first course and the meat then served as a flavoursome second course, or it can even be cooled and reserved for a separate meal.

1 Cut half the Pecorino cheese into small cubes. Grate the remaining cheese. Mix together the grated and cubed cheese in a bowl. Add the garlic and parsley, then stir in the chilli powder and nutmeg.

2 Lay the meat on a board and cover it with clear film (plastic wrap), tucking the wrap under the board to secure it. Using a meat mallet, flatten the meat as much as possible, taking care not to tear it.

3 Unwrap the meat and trim off any fat or gristle. The piece of meat should be fairly even, relatively thin and capable of being rolled.

4 Cover the flattened meat completely with pancetta slices, top with the cheese mixture, sprinkle with salt and carefully roll it up. Secure the roll with kitchen string (twine).

5 Heat the lard or dripping with the oil in a deep frying pan or casserole. Seal the meat roll on all sides, then pour in the wine. Cook for 3 minutes, turning the meat frequently, to boil off the alcohol.

6 Add the tomatoes to the pan, sprinkle with a little salt and cover tightly. Simmer very slowly for about 3 hours, adding a little water occasionally.

7 Bring a large pan of lightly salted water to the boil. Add the pasta and return to the boil. Cook for 2–3 minutes until the pasta has risen to the surface of the water and is just tender. Drain well.

8 Remove the meat roll from the sauce and either keep it hot to serve as a second course, or allow it cool for serving as part of a separate meal.

9 Add the pasta to the sauce, toss well together, then transfer to a heated platter and serve, scattered with extra grated Pecorino, if you like.

PER PORTION Energy 327kcal/1362kJ; Protein 28.3g; Carbohydrate 5.3g, of which sugars 4.5g; Fat 20.7g, of which saturates 7.1g; Cholesterol 84mg; Calcium 136mg; Fibre 2g; Sodium 334mg.

SERVES 6

50g/2oz Pecorino cheese, plus extra to serve (optional)
2 garlic cloves, chopped
45ml/3 tbsp chopped fresh parsley
1.5ml/¼ tsp chilli powder
1.5ml/¼ tsp freshly grated nutmeg
1 large slice pork or beef, about 600g/1lb 6oz (see Cook's Tips)
75g/3oz finely sliced pancetta
30ml/2 tbsp lard, white cooking fat or dripping
45ml/3 tbsp olive oil
75ml/5 tbsp dry white wine
2 x 400g/14oz cans chopped tomatoes, drained and seeded
500g/1lb 6oz fresh pasta
sea salt

COOK'S TIPS

• This dish works best when the meat is in one piece. Beef skirt is excellent for this purpose, or use a skinned and boned shoulder of pork.
• The meat roll is also delicious served cold.

RICE AND AUBERGINE BAKE
RISO E MELANZANE ALLA PALERMITANA

The shiny purple aubergine is the most popular vegetable in Sicily and has been ever since the Arabs introduced it to the island. It is used in everything from antipasti to desserts. This recipe may seem slightly long-winded, but it is definitely worth all the effort as the finished result looks and tastes spectacular.

SERVES 8

3 large aubergines (eggplants)
2 onions
50g/2oz/¼ cup unsalted butter
90ml/6 tbsp olive oil, plus extra
   for greasing
30ml/2 tbsp chopped fresh parsley
8 fresh basil leaves, torn into shreds
275g/10oz tomatoes, peeled,
   seeded and cut in quarters
275g/10oz/1½ cups risotto rice
600ml/1 pint/2½ cups hot chicken
   or vegetable stock
45ml/3 tbsp plain (all-purpose) flour
sunflower oil, for shallow frying
115g/4oz/1 cup grated Caciocavallo
   cheese (see Variation)
sea salt and ground black pepper

VARIATIONS

• Use grated Provolone or mozzarella cheese instead of Caciocavallo, if necessary.
• This dish tastes just as good served cold the next day.

1 Trim the aubergines and slice them into rounds 2cm/¾ inch thick. Spread them out in a colander and sprinkle generously with salt. Stand the colander in the sink, fit a plate inside to cover the aubergines, put a weight on top and leave to drain for 1–2 hours.

2 Meanwhile, peel the onions and put them in a pan. Cover with water, bring to the boil and cook for 10 minutes. Drain. Cool for 4–5 minutes, then slice thinly.

3 Melt the butter with half the olive oil in a pan. Add half the sliced onion and fry for 4–5 minutes until softened. Stir in the parsley and basil. Cook for 5 minutes, then stir in the tomatoes. Season with salt and pepper, cover and simmer for 20 minutes, stirring occasionally.

4 Preheat the oven to 190°C/375°F/Gas 5. Heat the rest of the oil in a flameproof casserole. Add the remaining onion and fry for 4 minutes until transparent.

5 Stir in the rice until shiny and coated in oil, then stir in the stock. Cover the casserole with a lid or foil and put it in the oven. Bake for 15 minutes.

6 Meanwhile, rinse the aubergine slices and pat them dry with kitchen paper. Dust them lightly with flour. Heat the sunflower oil in a frying pan until sizzling.

7 Fry the aubergine slices in batches for 3 minutes on each side or until golden brown. Add more oil to the pan as needed between batches. Lift out the aubergine slices with a slotted spoon and drain on kitchen paper.

8 Take the rice mixture out of the oven and stir in 30–45ml/2–3 tbsp of grated Caciocavallo cheese.

9 Grease a 1.2kg/2½lb round mould with oil, then line the base and sides with aubergine slices. Cover with a layer of the tomato sauce, then with a layer of rice, and then a generous sprinkling of grated Caciocavallo. Continue in this way until the mould is full, banging it down firmly on the work surface every now and again to settle the ingredients. Finish with a sprinkling of cheese.

10 Bake for 10 minutes, then remove from the oven and turn out on to a platter. Serve immediately.

PER PORTION Energy 371kcal/1544kJ; Protein 8.4g; Carbohydrate 38.6g, of which sugars 5.6g; Fat 20.2g, of which saturates 7.8g; Cholesterol 28mg; Calcium 152mg; Fibre 2.9g; Sodium 158mg.

SERVES 4 TO 6

juice of ½ lemon
12 medium artichokes
75ml/5 tbsp olive oil
1 garlic clove
175ml/6fl oz/¾ cup dry white wine
350g/12oz/1⅔ cups Arborio rice
2 sachets powdered saffron or
    1 pinch saffron threads, soaked
    in 45ml/3 tbsp hot water
200g/7oz thick-cut prosciutto
    crudo, cubed
2 eggs
100g/3½oz/scant 1 cup grated
    Pecorino cheese
sea salt and ground black pepper

FOR THE SAUCE
75g/3oz/6 tbsp unsalted butter
25g/1oz/¼ cup plain
    (all-purpose) flour
600ml/1 pint/2½ cups warm milk
pinch of freshly grated nutmeg
pinch of sea salt

RICE AND ARTICHOKE TIMBALE
TIMBALLO DI RISO E CARCIOFI

This elegant dish from Puglia is delicious and simple to make, once the fiddly business of preparing the artichokes has been done. They need to be stripped right back and then carefully trimmed down to the bases, removing every trace of the furry choke. The ham should be cut quite thickly, but not so thickly that it becomes chewy.

1 To make the sauce, melt the butter in a pan and stir in the flour. Gradually add the warm milk, whisking constantly to prevent lumps. Stir in nutmeg and salt to taste and simmer gently for about 15 minutes, stirring constantly, until the sauce is thick enough to coat the back of a spoon. Remove the pan from the heat and cover the surface of the sauce with a little cold water to prevent a skin from forming. Set aside.

2 Fill a bowl with water and add the lemon juice. Clean and trim the artichokes and add them to the acidulated water.

3 Heat the olive oil in a pan and add the garlic. Fry for about 3 minutes. Meanwhile, drain the artichokes and slice them thinly. Add to the pan and fry for 5 minutes, turning them occasionally.

4 Add the wine and season with salt and pepper. Simmer the artichokes for 30 minutes, or until they are very soft. Add water as needed.

5 Meanwhile, bring a pan of lightly salted water to the boil. Add the rice. Cook over a medium heat for 10 minutes, then add the saffron. Cook for a further 2 minutes, until just tender.

6 Drain the rice and spread it out in a large bowl. Let it cool slightly, then add the ham, eggs, cheese and sauce, and mix well. Line a 1.5 litre/2½ pint/6 cup baking dish or mould with baking parchment. Preheat the oven to 200°C/400°F/Gas 6.

7 Spoon two-thirds of the rice mixture into the baking dish or mould and pat it evenly on to the base and sides to form a case or shell. Spoon most of the artichokes into the centre. Cover with the remaining rice. Level the surface.

8 Bake for 30 minutes, then remove the timbale from the oven and let it cool for a few minutes before turning it out of the mould. Spoon the reserved artichokes around the base and serve.

PER PORTION Energy 604kcal/2516kJ; Protein 23.2g; Carbohydrate 55.9g, of which sugars 6.2g; Fat 30g, of which saturates 13.4g; Cholesterol 134mg; Calcium 381mg; Fibre 0.9g; Sodium 795mg.

RISOTTO WITH STOCKFISH
RISOTTO CON LO STOCCO

Stocco is dried stockfish: a medium-size cod that has been hung on wooden scaffolding to dry in the sun, then expertly salted and air dried. To transform this hard, unappetizing product into something edible, the fish must be cleaned and soaked in good quality tap water. The water that flows from the Apennine springs in the area of Mammola is said to be perfect for the task, and this, together with the skill of the local craftsmen, has given Calabrian stocco the reputation of being the finest in Italy.

1 Melt the butter in a large heavy pan, add the onion and fry over a medium heat for 5 minutes or until golden brown. Meanwhile, set the stock simmering in a separate pan.

2 Stir the flaked stockfish into the onion, then add the wine and stir over the heat until the alcohol evaporates. Add the rice and toast the grains for 2–3 minutes, stirring constantly to prevent them from scorching.

3 When the rice is crackling hot, start adding the hot stock, one or two ladlefuls at a time. Stir constantly and do not ladle in more stock until the previous amount has been absorbed.

4 After about 20 minutes, when the rice grains are soft and plump, stir in the oil and the parsley. Take the pan off the heat, cover it with a lid and set aside for 3–4 minutes, then stir again gently and serve.

SERVES 4

25g/1oz/2 tbsp unsalted butter
1 onion, finely chopped
1.5 litres/2½ pints/6 cups fish stock
   (preferably made with trimmings
   from the dried fish)
500g/1¼lb stockfish or dried salt
   cod, soaked, washed and flaked
175ml/6fl oz/¾ cup dry white wine
350g/12oz/1⅔ cups risotto rice
30ml/2 tbsp extra virgin olive oil
a handful of fresh flat leaf parsley,
   finely chopped

COOK'S TIP

As with all risottos, it is important to add the stock gradually. Stir constantly and only add more liquid when the spoon leaves a clear wake behind it as it is drawn through the grains of rice.

PER PORTION Energy 565kcal/2361kJ; Protein 30.3g; Carbohydrate 76g, of which sugars 4.5g; Fat 12.1g, of which saturates 4.3g; Cholesterol 72mg; Calcium 52mg; Fibre 1.1g; Sodium 126mg.

FISH AND SHELLFISH
PESCE E FRUTTI
DI MARE

All over the southern regions, as in the rest of Italy, fish and shellfish are highly prized and form an essential part of the local diet. With such a huge variety of freshly caught fish and shellfish available, and plenty of dried baccalà (salt cod) or stoccafisso (stockfish) as a backup, the local recipes for fish are almost too numerous to count. With the possible exception of Puglia, where lamb and mutton are abundant thanks to the shepherding trade, fish and shellfish tend to take precedence over meat and poultry as the main protein source in these southern regions. As well as a shared overall enjoyment of fish in general, each region of the south has their own preferred varieties of fish or shellfish, which appear time and time again in the profusion of wonderful local recipes.

MUSSELS, SQUID AND SWORDFISH STEAKS

Over time, Calabria and Sicily have become intrinsically associated with the two giants of the sea, tuna and swordfish, which swim the waters of the Messina Strait. Countless recipes for their preparation exist, and the locals are experts at picking and choosing the best specimens.

The mattanza (the slaughter) is an ancient and traditional method of fishing for tuna, developed in the waters around Trapani, Sicily. Each April, the fishermen place a number of intricate net systems in the water, spreading up to 5 kms/3 miles, that trap the tuna. In May, the boats participate in the ritual of the mattanza, surrounding the trapped fish and drawing the tuna together and towards the surface so that they can be harpooned. This apparently renders the meat of the tuna more tender, although this ancient custom of fishing is gradually disappearing due to increased global awareness of the importance of fish sustainability and animal rights.

Most of Basilicata is mountainous and stretches inland, although the pretty little coastal resort of Maratea is famous for its fresh fish, and provides this region with its own repertoire of fish dishes.

Puglia's long coastline means there is absolutely no shortage of fish and shellfish along whole length of the region. There is a particular fondness for raw mussels, clams and other shellfish in and around the Bari area, bravely eaten with just a squeeze of lemon.

Squid plays a big part in the southern fish menu as it is relatively easy to catch and available all year around. Also cheap and readily available are mussels, which are used in countless recipes including the ubiquitous fish stew, which exists in all four of these regions with slight local variations.

BAKED STUFFED SARDINES
SARDE A BECCAFICO

Beccafico, literally translated from the Italian as 'pecker of figs', are little birds that like to hang by their feet from ripe figs and peck away at the sweet flesh. You might see a resemblance between them and the stuffed sardines, with their rounded bellies and beak-like tails. This particular recipe comes from the eastern side of Sicily.

1 Preheat the oven to 180°C/350°F/Gas 4. If using fresh sardines, slit them along the belly and remove the innards with your fingers while holding them under running water. Place each sardine flat on its back, tail pointing towards you. Twist off the head by pulling it towards you so that it comes away with the spine and other bones, leaving the tail intact.

2 Drain the sultanas and pat them dry with kitchen paper. Put half the oil into a pan and add 15ml/1 tbsp of the breadcrumbs. Heat, stirring gently, so that the crumbs absorb the oil.

3 Remove the breadcrumbs from the heat and stir in the sultanas, pine nuts and parsley. Season the stuffing with pepper, then chop the anchovies finely and stir them into the mixture. Add salt if needed.

4 Using half the remaining oil, grease a baking dish that is large enough to hold all the fish in a single layer.

5 Insert stuffing into each of the fish. Depending upon the size of the sardines, you can either put the stuffing into the belly or wrap the flattened fish around the filling and roll them up. Secure with a cocktail stick (toothpick).

6 Arrange the stuffed sardines in the dish with their tails pointing upwards and the bay leaves tucked in between the fish. Drizzle with the remaining oil and scatter over the remaining breadcrumbs.

7 Bake for 30 minutes and serve immediately or allow to cool. Sardines cooked this way are delicious hot or cold.

SERVES 4

800g/1¾lb fresh sardines or thawed
   frozen sardines
50g/2oz/⅓ cup sultanas (golden
   raisins), soaked in warm water
   for 15 minutes
120ml/4fl oz/½ cup olive oil
60ml/4 tbsp fresh white breadcrumbs
50g/2oz/⅔ cup pine nuts
30ml/2 tbsp chopped fresh parsley
sea salt and ground black pepper
6 salted anchovies, rinsed, dried
   and boned
3–4 dried bay leaves

COOK'S TIP

This is best made with really fresh sardines, ideally straight from the sea, but you can use thawed frozen fish if you can't get fresh fish.

PER PORTION Energy 596kcal/2481kJ; Protein 36.1g; Carbohydrate 21.1g, of which sugars 9.8g; Fat 41.3g, of which saturates 6.8g; Cholesterol 0mg; Calcium 215mg; Fibre 1.3g; Sodium 467mg.

4 even-sized red mullet, total
    weight about 1kg/2¼lb, scaled
    and cleaned
20ml/4 tsp dried oregano
120ml/4fl oz/½ cup extra virgin
    olive oil
30ml/2 tbsp chopped fresh parsley
16 black olives, pitted
salt and ground black pepper

PER PORTION Energy 328kcal/1364kJ; Protein 24.5g;
Carbohydrate 0.4g, of which sugars 0.3g; Fat 25.5g,
of which saturates 2.9g; Cholesterol 0mg;
Calcium 123mg; Fibre 1g; Sodium 411mg.

RED MULLET IN A PARCEL
TRIGLIE AL CARTOCCIO

Baking fresh fish in a parcel of baking parchment or foil is a cooking method used
to great effect all over Italy. It has the benefit of retaining all the wonderful flavour
of the fish and preventing it from drying out during the cooking process. This is
a recipe from Puglia, and like most dishes from this region, it uses very few
ingredients. Mullet is quite bony, but it is so delicious cooked in this way that it
is worth braving the bones for the magnificent meaty flavour.

1 Preheat the oven to 200°C/400°F/Gas 6.
Rinse the mullet thoroughly and pat them dry
with kitchen paper. Season generously inside
and out, and sprinkle 5ml/1 tsp oregano
inside each fish.

2 Oil four large squares of baking parchment
or foil. Place a fish on each and sprinkle with
the parsley. Arrange four olives on each fish.

3 Sprinkle with the remaining olive oil. Bring
up the sides of the foil or parchment and twist
or fold to enclose the fish completely.

4 Place the parcels in a large roasting pan.
Bake for 30 minutes.

5 Place each parcel on a plate for unwrapping
at the table, and serve immediately.

SERVES 4

1 large gilthead bream, cleaned and
   scaled, about 1kg/2¼lb
500g/1¼lb potatoes
150ml/¼ pint/⅔ cup extra virgin
   olive oil, plus extra for basting
a handful of fresh flat leaf
   parsley, chopped
4 garlic cloves, finely chopped
75g/3oz Pecorino cheese, grated
sea salt and ground black pepper

PUGLIESE BAKED BREAM
ORATA ALLA PUGLIESE

The fish for this dish is cooked on a base of sliced potatoes that has been flavoured with garlic, fresh parsley and grated Pecorino. The cheese needs to be really pungent and peppery, so choose one that is mature and full of flavour. Serve this dish with a green salad and some slow-roasted tomatoes for a really fantastic meal.

1 Preheat the oven to 200°C/400°F/Gas 6. Rinse the fish thoroughly and pat it dry.

2 Peel the potatoes, slice them about 1cm/½in thick and place them in a bowl of cold water. Leave to soak until required.

3 Use half of the oil to coat the fish generously, both inside and out. Season with salt and pepper and tuck half the parsley and garlic into the cavity.

4 Drain the potatoes and rub the slices dry in a clean cloth.

5 Put the potatoes into a baking dish that is large enough to hold the fish. Add the rest of the oil with the remaining parsley and garlic. Mix well. Spread the potatoes evenly in the dish, season them with salt and pepper, then sprinkle with the cheese.

6 Lay the fish on top of the potatoes. Bake for about 40 minutes or until the potatoes are tender and the fish is cooked through, basting occasionally with a little olive oil.

7 Serve the fish and potatoes immediately, straight from the baking dish.

VARIATION

Although traditionally this dish uses a gilthead or emperor bream, any large, thick fish could be substituted instead, provided it will cook in more or less the same time as the potatoes.

PER PORTION Energy 456kcal/1894kJ; Protein 31.8g; Carbohydrate 0.4g, of which sugars 0.3g; Fat 36.5g, of which saturates 7.4g; Cholesterol 19mg; Calcium 340mg; Fibre 0.6g; Sodium 334mg.

CALABRIAN BAKED SWORDFISH
PESCE SPADA ARRAGANATO

The perfect accompaniment for this delicious swordfish dish is a platter of grilled vegetables such as peppers, courgettes, carrots, red onion slices and aubergines. For baking the fish, use a dish that will hold all the fish steaks snugly side by side, and make sure they are completely sandwiched in the breadcrumb mixture, as this will help to keep the swordfish moist.

1 Rinse and dry the swordfish steaks. Preheat the oven to 180°C/350°F/Gas 4.

2 Put the breadcrumbs in a bowl and add the grated cheese and parsley. Season with salt and pepper to taste and mix well.

3 Use a little of the olive oil to grease a baking dish which is just large enough to hold the steaks snugly in one layer. Brush the steaks with oil on both sides.

4 Spread half the breadcrumb mixture over the base of the dish, and lay the swordfish steaks on top. Season the fish with salt and pepper.

5 Cover with the rest of the breadcrumb mixture, then drizzle with the remaining oil.

6 Bake for 10 minutes, then take the dish out of the oven, pour the lemon juice evenly over the crumb topping and return to the oven for 10 minutes more. Serve immediately.

SERVES 4

4 thick swordfish steaks, about
    175g/6oz each
225g/8oz/4 cups soft white
    breadcrumbs
150g/5oz Pecorino cheese, grated
45ml/3 tbsp finely chopped fresh
    flat leaf parsley
90ml/6 tbsp extra virgin olive oil
juice of 1 lemon
sea salt and ground black pepper

VARIATIONS
....

• Use tuna steaks instead of swordfish, adjusting the cooking times if necessary, depending upon the thickness of the fish.
• Flavour the breadcrumb topping by adding some chopped olives and rinsed and chopped capers.

PER PORTION Energy 737kcal/3089kJ; Protein 57.4g; Carbohydrate 43.9g, of which sugars 1.8g; Fat 38g, of which saturates 11.9g; Cholesterol 118mg; Calcium 557mg; Fibre 1.9g; Sodium 1103mg.

CALABRIAN TUNA STEAKS
TONNO ALLA CALABRESE

This recipe typifies Calabrian cuisine and brings together many of the ingredients that are most closely identified with the region. The flavours work very well together, making the most of the taste of fresh tuna and creating a satisfying dish, with just enough chilli to add a hint of fire.

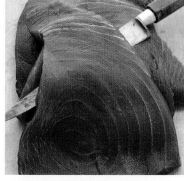

1 Rinse the tuna steaks in cold water, drain and pat dry. Season the steaks thoroughly on both sides with salt and pepper.

2 Heat half the olive oil in a frying pan large enough to hold the tuna steaks in a single layer. Coat the steaks lightly in flour, add them to the pan and fry them over a medium heat for 3 minutes on each side.

3 Sprinkle with the wine and allow the alcohol to boil off for 1 minute.

4 Using a spatula, lift out the fish and drain on kitchen paper. Place on a plate and spoon over the pan juices.

5 Heat the remaining oil in the pan. Add the pancetta, garlic, onion and half the parsley. Fry gently for 5 minutes, stirring occasionally.

6 Add the anchovy fillets and mash them into the hot mixture with a fork. After 1 minute, stir in the tomatoes. Add the chilli and simmer over very low heat for 15 minutes.

7 Slide the tuna steaks back into the pan and spoon some of the tomato mixture over them. Heat through thoroughly for about 8 minutes, turning them over gently once.

8 Serve the tuna immediately topped with the sauce and sprinkled with the remaining parsley.

SERVES 4

4 even-sized fresh tuna steaks,
    total weight about 800g/1¾lb
60ml/4 tbsp olive oil
30ml/2 tbsp plain (all-purpose) flour
60ml/4 tbsp dry white wine
50g/2oz pancetta, chopped
1 large garlic clove, chopped
1 onion, chopped
30ml/2 tbsp chopped fresh parsley
4 anchovy fillets in oil, drained
    and boned
400g/14oz can chopped
    tomatoes, drained
½ dried red chilli, chopped
sea salt and ground black pepper

PER PORTION Energy 472kcal/1976kJ; Protein 51.7g; Carbohydrate 10.2g, of which sugars 4.2g; Fat 24.2g, of which saturates 5.1g; Cholesterol 64mg; Calcium 64mg; Fibre 1.5g; Sodium 380mg.

800g/1¾lb salt cod
75ml/5 tbsp extra virgin olive oil
275g/10oz bottled roasted red (bell)
    peppers, drained
3 garlic cloves, chopped
3 dried red chillies, chopped
a handful of fresh flat leaf
    parsley, chopped
sea salt (optional)

VARIATIONS

• Fresh fish can be used for
this dish, but because it has a
much more delicate taste than
salt cod, the quantity of chilli
should be reduced.
• Reconstituted dried red (bell)
peppers can be used instead
of bottled roasted peppers.

PER PORTION Energy 207kcal/861kJ; Protein 25.1g;
Carbohydrate 3.2g, of which sugars 3g; Fat 10.4g,
of which saturates 1.5g; Cholesterol 61mg;
Calcium 32mg; Fibre 1.2g; Sodium 85mg.

SALT COD WITH RED PEPPERS
BACCALÀ E PEPERONI

Fiery and full of flavour, this winter dish comes from Basilicata, and was created for
that time of year when there is a shortage of fresh vegetables and rough seas mean
fish is in short supply. Salt fish needs to be soaked before cooking, so allow for this
when planning when to serve the dish.

1 Soak the salt cod in enough cold water to
cover for 24 hours, changing the water often.
Drain well.

2 Trim the fish, removing any obvious bones,
and put it in a pan. Pour over cold water to
cover and heat to simmering. Cook for about
8 minutes until the fish is soft.

3 Drain well and remove the skin. Flake the
cod, removing any remaining bones.

4 Heat the oil in a pan and add the roasted
peppers, garlic, chillies and parsley. Fry over a
medium heat for about 10 minutes, stirring
frequently. Add a little water if necessary.

5 Add the flaked salt cod to the pan and mix
well. Taste and add salt if necessary, although
the fish may already be salty enough. Cook for
1–2 minutes to heat through.

6 Serve on a heated platter.

SERVES 4 TO 6

1kg/2¼lb stockfish, preferably
   Stocco di Mammola, soaked in
   water until soft
115g/4oz/2 cups soft white
   breadcrumbs
75g/3oz hard goat's cheese, grated
45ml/3 tbsp chopped fresh flat
   leaf parsley
1 dried red chilli, chopped
3 garlic cloves, finely chopped
2 eggs, beaten
60ml/4 tbsp olive oil
400g/14oz can chopped tomatoes
sea salt

CALABRIAN FISH PATTIES
POLPETTE DI STOCCO

These are the Calabrian version of fishcakes – hot and spicy with plenty of garlic and some grated goat's cheese for extra pungency. The fish that is traditionally used is stocco, or stockfish, which is a member of the cod family. It is dried, and then salted, as opposed to baccalà which is salted without being dried. Stockfish from Mammola in Calabria is recommended for this recipe, but another type of fish could be used instead, as long as it is robust enough to withstand the other flavours in the dish.

1 Drain the soaked stockfish, clean and trim it, then flake and chop it finely, removing any bones. Put it in a large bowl.

2 Add the breadcrumbs, cheese, parsley, chilli and half the garlic. Stir in the beaten eggs, mixing well.

3 Divide the mixture into 8–12 portions and shape into patties. Set aside.

4 Heat the olive oil in a large frying pan and add the remaining garlic. Fry over gentle heat for about 3 minutes. As soon as the garlic begins to brown, stir in the canned tomatoes. Simmer the sauce for 10 minutes.

5 Season with salt to taste, then add the stockfish patties and spoon the sauce over to coat. Cover the pan and simmer for 10–15 minutes until cooked, then serve hot.

COOK'S TIPS

• You may not need to add all the egg. Stir in enough to bind the mixture. It should be firm enough to shape into patties.
• Shaping the patties is easier if the mixture is lightly chilled, so put it into the refrigerator for 30 minutes, if you have time.
• For a less spicy mixture, do not use the dried chilli seeds.

PER PORTION Energy 346kcal/1450kJ; Protein 38.2g; Carbohydrate 17.3g, of which sugars 2.9g; Fat 14.2g, of which saturates 4g; Cholesterol 152mg; Calcium 87mg; Fibre 1.5g; Sodium 353mg.

PUGLIESE FISH STEW
ZUPPA DI PESCE PUGLIESE

This is a speciality of the large coastal city of Taranto, in Puglia. This important Italian port is home to wonderful seafood markets, which are filled with a remarkable array of fresh fish and shellfish. With so many varieties to choose from, local cooks will adapt the ingredients according to what is available at the time. This is the sort of dish that requires plenty of time to enjoy, as the seafood is only partially prepared and diners need to remove bones and shells at the table.

SERVES 8

1.3kg/3lb prepared seafood, such as a mixture of huss and cod (cut into chunks), small whole red mullet, squid, raw unshelled prawns (shrimp), mussels, razor clams and Venus clams
120ml/4fl oz/½ cup olive oil
3 garlic cloves, chopped
45ml/3 tbsp chopped fresh parsley
10 ripe tomatoes, peeled, seeded and sliced into strips
8 thick slices ciabatta bread
sea salt and ground black pepper

COOK'S TIPS

• Shellfish such as mussels and clams must be tightly closed when you start to cook them, and should open naturally when cooked. Never force a cooked mussel or clam open to eat it.
• Provide lemon slices, finger bowls and paper towels for guests as well as empty bowls for shells and bones.

PER PORTION Energy 500kcal/2108kJ; Protein 40.7g; Carbohydrate 54.5g, of which sugars 5.6g; Fat 14.7g, of which saturates 2.1g; Cholesterol 75mg; Calcium 153mg; Fibre 3.4g; Sodium 644mg.

1 Put the chunks of fish, whole small fish, squid and prawns in a large colander. Wash thoroughly under cold running water, then drain well.

2 Scrub the remaining shellfish and pull off the beards from the mussels. Discard any clams or mussels with broken shells or which gape open and do not close when tapped on the work top. Put the mussels and clams in separate bowls. Pour cold salted water over both. Leave to soak.

3 Heat half the oil in a large pan. Add the garlic, half the parsley and half the tomatoes. Fry for 5 minutes, then add the fish from the colander. Add 30–45ml/2–3 tbsp cold water and season. Lower the heat, cover and cook for 6–8 minutes.

4 Put all the mussels into a large shallow pan. Cover tightly and shake the pan over the heat for 6 minutes, or until all the mussels have opened. Discard any that have not opened. Strain the liquid from the mussels over the cooked fish. Put the mussels into a bowl.

5 Put the remaining oil into a large, heavy pan. Add the remaining parsley and tomatoes and fry gently for 5 minutes. Add the clams, stir, season, cover and cook for 6 minutes or until the shells have opened. Discard any that remain shut.

6 Toast the ciabatta and place a slice in each of eight soup bowls. Divide the cooked fish, with the liquid, among the bowls, scatter over the mussels, with their liquid, then the clams. Serve.

TRAPANI FISH COUSCOUS
CUSCUSU DI TRAPANI

This dish comes from Trapani, where the salt flats of Sicily glisten under the relentless sun. Couscous was introduced to the island centuries ago and was adopted so enthusiastically that it is now synonymous with Sicilian food. It is particularly popular in the west and on the outlying islets. Sicilian cooks often make couscous from scratch, using a special bowl called a maffaradda to roll the damp semolina into tiny balls. This is a time-consuming task, so it is easier to use ready-made couscous.

1 Put the saffron powder or threads in a bowl and pour over the hot water. Leave to stand for about 10 minutes.

2 Put the couscous in a large bowl. Strain in the saffron liquid, then mix into the couscous. Spread out the grains on a large tray and leave to dry while you cook the fish.

3 Heat half the olive oil in a large, deep pan. Add the chopped parsley and garlic. Fry gently for 5 minutes, then add the onion and bay leaf. Fry for 5 minutes more, then add the tomato. Level the mixture in the pan and lay the fish fillets on top, preferably in a single layer.

4 Season with salt and pepper and pour over water to cover. Simmer over low heat for 20 minutes or until the fish flakes easily when tested with the tip of a knife.

5 Using a slotted spoon, transfer the fish fillets to a board. When cool enough to handle, remove the skin and any remaining bones. Set the fish aside.

6 Strain the cooking liquid into a large bowl. Pour 475ml/15fl oz/2 cups into a measuring jug (cup) and set it aside. If you have any left over, take note of the amount, pour it into a large pan and top up with water to make 2 litres/3½ pints/8 cups. If no stock remains, just use water.

7 Place a large colander or sieve (strainer) over the pan containing the stock or water. Plug any gaps to prevent steam from escaping (see Cook's Tip). Add the couscous.

8 Stir the remaining 45ml/3 tbsp olive oil into the couscous. Cover the pan with a lid and then lay a thick, heavy cloth over the lid. Place over low heat and steam for about 40 minutes, or until the couscous is fluffy.

9 Reheat the reserved fish stock. Transfer the couscous to a bowl and lightly stir in half the hot fish stock. Cover with a lid and then wrap the bowl and the lid in the heavy cloth. Leave to stand while you gently reheat the fish in a separate pan with the remaining stock.

10 Unwrap the couscous. Stir in the cinnamon, nutmeg, salt and pepper. Serve it on a platter with the fish on top.

SERVES 8

3 sachets powdered saffron, or a
    large pinch of saffron threads
120ml/4fl oz/½ cup hot water
400g/14oz/2⅓ cups coarse couscous
90ml/6 tbsp olive oil
60ml/4 tbsp chopped fresh parsley
3 garlic cloves, chopped
1 onion, thinly sliced
1 dried bay leaf
1 tomato, peeled, seeded
    and quartered
1.2kg/2½lb mixed fish fillets, such as
    cod, eel, red mullet and John Dory
1.5ml/¼ tsp ground cinnamon
pinch of freshly grated nutmeg
sea salt and ground black pepper

COOK'S TIP

If your colander is narrower than the pan it sits upon, use a damp, clean dish towel to plug any gaps. It is important that no steam escapes during the cooking process.

PER PORTION Energy 315kcal/1315kJ; Protein 30.7g; Carbohydrate 26.7g, of which sugars 0.9g; Fat 10g, of which saturates 1.3g; Cholesterol 69mg; Calcium 43mg; Fibre 0.6g; Sodium 94mg.

STUFFED SQUID
SEPPIE RIPIENE

Elaborate recipes are rare in Puglia, where the tendency is to use just a few basic, but good-quality, ingredients. The squid for this delectable dish must be fresh and carefully cleaned, and the tomatoes need to be juicy and sweet.

1 Heat the olive oil in a wide, shallow pan that is large enough to hold all the squid in one layer. Add the garlic and fry over a medium heat for 5 minutes. Do not let it burn or it will taste bitter.

2 Chop the tomatoes, then add them to the pan. Season with salt and pepper to taste. Bring to the boil, then lower the heat and simmer for 30 minutes, stirring frequently and adding a little water if the sauce becomes dry.

3 Chop the squid tentacles and add them to the sauce. Remove from the heat and set aside.

4 Put the breadcrumbs in a bowl and add the cheese and enough of the beaten egg to bind the mixture. Mix the stuffing well.

5 Spoon the stuffing into the squid, dividing it evenly among them. The mixture will swell during cooking, so do not overfill the squid.

6 Either sew the stuffed squid closed using a darning needle threaded with fine cooking string (twine), or secure them with wooden cocktail sticks (toothpicks).

7 Lower the stuffed squid into the sauce, cover the pan and simmer very gently for about 1½ hours or until the squid are very tender, adding more water as required.

8 Season with salt and pepper, then serve either hot or cold, garnished with parsley, with crusty bread and a fresh green salad.

SERVES 4

60ml/4 tbsp olive oil
1 garlic clove, crushed
9 tomatoes, peeled and seeded
4 large squid, cleaned and ready
  to cook (see Cook's Tip)
60ml/4 tbsp dry breadcrumbs
60ml/4 tbsp grated Pecorino cheese
1 egg, beaten
sea salt and ground black pepper
chopped fresh parsley, to garnish

COOK'S TIP

To prepare a squid yourself, rinse it, then holding it firmly, grasp the tentacles and pull the head and entrails away from the body. Cut off the tentacles and set them aside. Discard the head, with the hard 'beak' and the ink sac. Peel the membrane from the body. Pull out and discard the 'quill'. Wash the body under cold running water, drain and dry it.

PER PORTION Energy 418kcal/1758kJ; Protein 37.7g; Carbohydrate 20.7g, of which sugars 7.4g; Fat 21.2g, of which saturates 5.9g; Cholesterol 456mg; Calcium 245mg; Fibre 2.6g; Sodium 508mg.

SERVES 4

1kg/2¼lb live mussels, scrubbed
  and bearded
75ml/5 tbsp olive oil
3 garlic cloves
600ml/l pint/2½ cups passata
  (bottled strained tomatoes) or
  sieved (strained) canned tomatoes
2 eggs, beaten
30ml/2 tbsp chopped fresh parsley
120ml/8 tbsp soft white breadcrumbs
a small handful of fresh basil, leaves
  torn into shreds
sea salt and ground black pepper

PER PORTION Energy 366kcal/1537kJ; Protein 21.2g;
Carbohydrate 29g, of which sugars 6.5g; Fat 19.3g,
of which saturates 3.1g; Cholesterol 125mg;
Calcium 238mg; Fibre 3g; Sodium 441mg.

STUFFED MUSSELS WITH TOMATO SAUCE
COZZE RIPIENE AL SUGO

This is a very tasty way to enjoy fresh mussels. Use the biggest shellfish you can find, as the preparation is more fiddly if the mussels are small. Clean them carefully, as any trace of grit or splinter of barnacle will spoil the effect of the whole dish.

1 Check the mussels, discarding any with damaged shells and any which are open and fail to close when tapped on the work surface.

2 Spread out the mussels in a wide frying pan. Cover the pan and place it over a fairly high heat. Shake the pan frequently. After about 6 minutes, all the mussels should have opened and yielded their liquid. Discard any that remain closed. Drain the mussels, reserving the liquid in the pan, and set them aside.

3 Heat the oil in a medium pan. Peel 2 garlic cloves and add them, whole, to the oil. Fry the garlic until it turns brown, then lift the cloves out with a slotted spoon and discard them.

4 Stir the passata or sieved tomatoes into the garlic-flavoured oil and season. Bring to the boil, then lower the heat, cover the pan and simmer the mixture for 20 minutes.

5 Meanwhile, make the stuffing. Chop the remaining garlic clove finely and put it in a bowl. Add the eggs, parsley and breadcrumbs. Season with salt and pepper.

6 Fill the empty half shell of each mussel with the stuffing, then close the shells around the mussels. Tie each one with a loop of kitchen string (twine) to keep the stuffing securely inside.

7 Strain the reserved liquid from the mussels and add it to the tomato sauce, with the basil.

8 Stir to mix, then add the mussels to the pan and spoon the sauce over them. Cover the pan tightly and simmer for 10 minutes.

9 Remove the string from the mussels and transfer them, with the sauce, to a heated platter. Serve immediately.

POULTRY, MEAT AND GAME

POLLAME, CARNE E CACCIA

On the menus of the deep south of Italy, meat is quite sparse. The traditional beef and veal of the north have a much smaller place in the culinary repertoire. In the forests and mountains of Basilicata or inland Calabria, local game features in dishes, including wild rabbit. While Calabrians hold a special place in their hearts for pork dishes, in Puglia it is traditionally mutton or lamb that makes up the collection of traditional meat dishes. In Sicily, meat and game rarely appear on the menu; it is largely vegetables, fish and beans that constitute the local menu, with pasta reigning supreme. A history of isolation and poverty in these regions led to cured pork becoming one of the main sources of meat, and almost all the local recipes reflect the use of this valuable source of protein. The addition of cheaper vegetables, such as carrots, onions and celery, adds flavour and bulk to meat dishes too.

CURED PORK AND
FLAVOURFUL STEWS

You are not very likely to be served the sophisticated veal dishes of northern Italy in any authentic local restaurants in Sicily or elsewhere in the south. At best, Pugliese cooking will offer up some rather basic, very rustic lamb stews, some of which have origins that are lost in the time of the traditional 'transumanza', long sheep trails that stretched the length of Puglia from l'Aquila at the northern end, to the golden city of Lecce at the very southern tip. Along the way, sheep that died of natural causes could be cooked and eaten, but of course the recipes created had to be practical enough to be cooked over open fires in all weathers, with very few ingredients or utensils. Very popular still is the rather dramatically grisly dish called Gnummeriddi, which consists purely of lamb guts, threaded on to sticks and grilled over a glowing fire. Eaten with just a sprinkling of salt and perhaps a little olive oil and lemon juice, it is not an easy dish to contemplate if one is not local!

Also worth mentioning is the black pig of Calabria, whose coarse, dense, tasty meat is largely cured and turned into sausages and bacon for the long winter months. Blood sausage is very popular in these parts. Known as Sanguinaccio, it is usually served as a soft, dark red sausage, but can sometimes also be the name for a local dessert made by beating the blood with sugar and chocolate until it coagulates. The resulting chocolate 'pudding' is served in a sundae dish with a blob of whipped cream and a glacé (candied) cherry.

Chicken, turkey and game feature occasionally on the local menus, served simply grilled or fried, or cooked in sustaining pies and hearty stews.

LUCANIAN CHICKEN PIE
LAKRUAR

Lucania was the ancient region of southern Italy which now comprises Basilicata. Nobody is sure of the origin of this ancient recipe. There is something vaguely North African about its composition, so maybe it was inspired by a Moroccan pastilla. Whatever its source, the combination of ingredients makes for a delectable pie.

1 Put the flour and salt in a large bowl and make a well in the centre. Mix the eggs, wine and oil in a jug (pitcher).

2 Add the mixture to the well in the flour with about 30ml/2 tbsp warm water. Mix with your hands, gradually incorporating the surrounding flour and adding more water as needed, to make a smooth, elastic dough. Cover the bowl and leave the dough to rest while you prepare the filling.

3 Skin the sausage and crumble the sausage meat into a bowl. Cut the chicken and cheese into small pieces. Add these to the sausage meat, then add the eggs and flavour with the cinnamon and a pinch of salt.

4 Preheat the oven to 200°C/400°F/Gas 6. Grease a shallow 20cm/8in pie dish.

5 On a lightly floured surface, roll out the pastry thinly and then cut out two rounds, the first one large enough to line the baking dish and the other, slightly smaller, for the top crust.

6 Use the first piece of pastry to line the dish and then trim the edges with a small, sharp knife.

7 Fill the lined dish with the chicken mixture and cover with the pastry lid. Seal the edges securely by pressing down on the rim with the tines of a fork. Trim away any excess pastry.

8 Using a sharp knife or metal skewer, pierce the surface of the pie in several places to let the steam escape during cooking. Sprinkle with cinnamon.

9 Bake for about 30 minutes, until the crust is crisp and golden. Serve the pie hot or cold, with a green salad, if you like.

SERVES 4 TO 6

500g/1¼lb/5 cups plain (all-purpose) flour
pinch of salt
2 eggs, beaten
90ml/6 tbsp dry white wine
90ml/6 tbsp extra virgin olive oil

FOR THE FILLING
1 Italian sausage
275g/10oz cooked chicken, preferably boiled or steamed
275g/10oz soft Tumma cheese
2 eggs
large pinch of ground cinnamon, plus extra for sprinkling
pinch of salt

VARIATION

Tumma is a cheese local to the south of Italy, and may be difficult to find, even in other parts of the country. Made from sheep's milk, this stretched curd cheese is useful for cooking because it melts slowly. A good alternative would be unsmoked Scamorza. Mozzarella can also be used, but the flavour will be much milder.

PER PORTION Energy 670kcal/2808kJ; Protein 27g; Carbohydrate 66.3g, of which sugars 1.6g; Fat 33.9g, of which saturates 13g; Cholesterol 191mg; Calcium 196mg; Fibre 2.7g; Sodium 329mg.

CALABRIAN TURKEY STEAKS WITH LIME
FESA DI TACCHINO AL CEDRO

Citrus fruits such as limes, bergamots and grapefruit grow profusely all over Calabria. Limes are an important feature of this simple, summery dish, which is delicious with a potato salad. For colour, serve it with some sliced tomatoes, dressed with oil, salt and torn basil leaves.

1 Place the turkey steaks between sheets of clear film (plastic wrap) and beat them with a meat mallet or rolling pin until they are as thin as possible.

2 Spread them out in a shallow dish and sprinkle with the oregano. Drizzle with the lime juice and half the olive oil and season with salt and pepper. Cover and leave to marinate at room temperature for about 1 hour.

3 Lift out the turkey slices and pat them dry with kitchen paper.

4 Pour the remaining olive oil into a frying pan. Add the garlic and heat over a high heat. When it sizzles, add as many of the turkey slices as the pan will hold in a single layer. Fry quickly, for only 1–2 minutes on each side, until cooked through.

5 Transfer the turkey to heated plates and keep hot while cooking the remaining slices.

6 Divide the juices remaining in the pan among the turkey slices, spooning them over the top. Garnish with the lime wedges and serve.

SERVES 4

600g/1lb 6oz thin turkey steaks
10ml/2 tsp dried oregano
3 ripe limes, 2 juiced and 1 sliced
    into wedges
1 garlic clove
75ml/5 tbsp extra virgin
    olive oil
sea salt and ground black pepper

VARIATIONS

• Orange or lemon juice could be used instead of lime.
• Instead of turkey steaks, try escalopes (US scallops) of chicken or veal, or thin slices of monkfish.
• Add finely grated lime rind to the marinade for extra flavour.

PER PORTION Energy 310kcal/1294kJ; Protein 32.9g; Carbohydrate 0.1g, of which sugars 0.1g; Fat 19.8g, of which saturates 3.4g; Cholesterol 92mg; Calcium 17mg; Fibre 0.1g; Sodium 82mg.

400g/14oz can plum tomatoes
in tomato juice
60ml/4 tbsp olive oil
12 fresh basil leaves,
coarsely shredded
50g/2oz/½ cup preserved
mushrooms in olive oil
50g/2oz/½ cup preserved
artichoke hearts in olive oil
8 pork rib chops
sea salt and ground black pepper

VARIATION

Although it is usual to serve
the sauce with meaty rib chops,
cooked on a grill (broiler) or
barbecue, it is also delicious
with grilled Italian sausages
or other grilled meats.

PER PORTION Energy 484kcal/2012kJ; Protein 29g;
Carbohydrate 3.2g, of which sugars 3.1g; Fat 39.7g,
of which saturates 10.6g; Cholesterol 99mg;
Calcium 30mg; Fibre 1.1g; Sodium 157mg.

PORK RIBS WITH MUSHROOMS AND ARTICHOKES
COSTE DI MAIALE ALLA SILANA

The rough-textured sauce served with the ribs comes from the high Sila mountain of
Calabria. It uses preserved mushrooms and artichokes, which is very fitting, considering
that the area is famous for bottling and salting these regional products, or preserving
them in oil. The sauce can be served separately, or poured over the meat.

1 Drain the canned tomatoes, reserving the
juice. Remove the seeds and chop the
tomatoes roughly.

2 Heat the oil in a pan and add the tomatoes.
Fry over medium heat for 15 minutes, stirring
frequently and adding a little of the reserved
juice if necessary to prevent the mixture from
sticking to the pan.

3 Season with salt and pepper and add the
basil leaves. Simmer for 15 minutes more,
stirring from time to time.

4 Preheat the grill (broiler) or prepare a
barbecue.

5 Chop the mushrooms and the artichoke
hearts finely.

6 Add the chopped mushrooms and
artichokes, with most of their oil, to the
tomato sauce. Stir well and leave the sauce
over a low heat while you cook the rib chops.

7 Place the chops on a rack under the hot grill
or on the barbecue. Cook for 2 minutes on each
side, then lower the heat or move the chops
to a cooler part of the barbecue and cook for
8 minutes more or until done to your liking.

8 Divide the chops among four warmed
plates, pour the sauce over and serve at once.

SERVES 4 TO 6

2 slices day-old bread, total weight about 115g/4oz
120ml/4fl oz/½ cup extra virgin olive oil
½ onion, chopped
1 garlic clove, chopped
400g/14oz passata (bottled strained tomatoes)
200g/7oz/scant 1 cup minced (ground) pork
200g/7oz/scant 1 cup minced (ground) beef
2 eggs, beaten
30ml/2 tbsp chopped fresh flat leaf parsley
50g/2oz/½ cup grated Pecorino cheese
30–45ml/2–3 tbsp wine must or sweet balsamic vinegar (see Cook's Tip)
75g/3oz/¾ cup flaked (sliced) almonds
sea salt and ground black pepper

CALABRIAN SWEET AND SOUR MEATBALLS
POLPETTE IN AGRODOLCE

There is plenty of texture and flavour in this wonderful Calabrian dish, which is capable of infinite variety. Although it usually consists of little meatballs, the mixture can also be made as one large meatloaf. The proportion of pork and beef can be altered, or just one meat can be used. The cheese, too, can be varied. The tomato sauce is delicious, but it can be omitted, and the meatballs simply fried, covered with wine must, spiked with almonds and served with boiled potatoes.

1 Soak the bread in water until soft. Heat about a quarter of the olive oil in a large pan and fry the onion and garlic for 3–4 minutes until the onion has softened.

2 Pour in the passata, mix well, season with salt and pepper and leave to simmer while you prepare the meatballs.

3 Put the pork and beef in a bowl and mix well, preferably with your hands. Add the eggs.

4 Drain the bread, squeeze it dry and mix the bread and eggs with the meat. Add the parsley and grated cheese, with salt and pepper to taste.

5 Work the mixture with your hands until all the ingredients are well distributed. Shape this mixture into little balls.

6 Heat the remaining oil in a large frying pan and shallow-fry the meatballs for about 5 minutes, until browned all over. Using tongs or a slotted spoon, transfer them to the tomato sauce and continue to cook for 10 minutes.

7 Remove the pan from the heat. Pour over the wine must. Leave to stand for 2–3 minutes.

8 Spoon the meatballs and sauce on to a heated serving platter and slip a few almond flakes into each meatball before serving.

COOK'S TIP

Wine must is wine that has just begun to ferment. It is sold in good Italian food shops, but if you can't find it, use a good-quality, sweet balsamic vinegar instead. To make regular balsamic vinegar sweet and sticky, boil it fast in a wide pan for about 15 minutes, or until sticky and reduced by about half. Cool and return to the bottle to use as normal.

PER PORTION Energy 442kcal/1837kJ; Protein 23.1g; Carbohydrate 13.4g, of which sugars 3.8g; Fat 33.4g, of which saturates 8.2g; Cholesterol 116mg; Calcium 189mg; Fibre 2.4g; Sodium 275mg.

MEATBALL AND RICOTTA BAKE
TRUSCELLO DI MESSINA

Truscello is a delicious, very light dish made up of tiny balls of clove-scented ricotta and beef, layered in a dish, bathed in stock and poached in the oven. The preparation is a bit fiddly but well worth the effort. It comes from Messina, which is the third largest city on the island of Sicily.

1 Put the beef in a large bowl. Season well with salt and pepper, then add 30ml/2 tbsp of the Parmesan cheese with the breadcrumbs and parsley. Beat 2 of the eggs lightly and add them to the bowl.

2 Using wet, clean hands, mix the ingredients together. Add a little stock if necessary, to bind the mixture, but not too much as it should be firm, not sloppy.

3 Pinch off small pieces of the mixture and roll into tiny meatballs, no larger than big olives.

4 Pour the stock into a large pan and bring to the boil. Lower the heat to a simmer and then add the meatballs. Simmer for no more than 3 minutes.

5 Lift the meatballs out with a slotted spoon and put them on a dish. Set aside to cool. Leave the stock over a low heat. Preheat the oven to 200°C/400°F/Gas 6.

6 Put the ricotta in a bowl and add the remaining Parmesan cheese. Beat the remaining eggs lightly and add them to the bowl with the ground cloves. Season.

7 Shape the ricotta mixture into balls the same size as the meatballs. The ricotta needs to be really dry and stiff – if the mixture is too sloppy, add more breadcrumbs and Parmesan until you can shape it into balls with ease.

8 Pour a little of the hot stock into a 1.5-litre/2½-pint/6-cup baking dish. Cover with a layer of ricotta balls, then with a layer of meatballs.

9 Pour over stock to just cover, then layer the ricotta balls and meatballs on top. Continue in this way until the final layer of meatballs has been added. Pour over the remaining stock.

10 Bake for 5–10 minutes, so that the meat and cheese balls heat through but the ricotta does not melt. Serve immediately.

SERVES 4 TO 6

275g/10oz/1¼ cups very lean
   minced (ground) beef
115g/4oz/1⅓ cups freshly grated
   Parmesan cheese, plus extra
   if needed
115g/4oz/2 cups stale white
   breadcrumbs, plus extra if needed
45ml/3 tbsp chopped fresh parsley
5 eggs
500ml/17fl oz/generous 2 cups
   strongly-flavoured beef stock
275g/10oz drained fresh
   ricotta cheese
1.5ml/¼ tsp ground cloves
sea salt and ground black pepper

COOK'S TIP

To prevent the meat and ricotta balls from disintegrating, and the dish from becoming sloppy, use crumbs from bread that is at least a day old, ricotta cheese that is very dry and crumbly, and very lean beef.

PER PORTION Energy 380kcal/1590kJ; Protein 29.5g; Carbohydrate 16.5g, of which sugars 2.1g; Fat 22.4g, of which saturates 11.3g; Cholesterol 223mg; Calcium 300mg; Fibre 0.8g; Sodium 457mg.

PUGLIESE BEEF ROLLS
BRACIOLINE

This traditional dish from Puglia consists of stuffed beef rolls stewed in a flavoursome tomato sauce. It is generally served over pasta, although the rolls can also be served as a main course accompanied by potatoes and vegetables.

1 Make the tomato sauce. Heat 60ml/4 tbsp of the oil in a heavy pan and add the chopped vegetables. Fry over a low heat for 10 minutes until the vegetables are soft and the onion is transparent. Add the tomatoes and stir well. Cover and simmer for 30 minutes, stirring often.

2 Meanwhile, lay one of the meat slices on a board and cover with clear film (plastic wrap), tucking the film under the board. Using a meat mallet or a rolling pin, beat the meat until really thin, being careful not to tear it.

3 Remove the clear film and place a slice of prosciutto over the flattened beef slice. Add a sprinkling of parsley, a little black pepper and an eighth of the grated cheese.

4 Roll the meat up tightly to enclose the filling and secure the roll with a wooden cocktail stick (toothpick) or a piece of kitchen string (twine). Make the remaining rolls in the same way.

5 Heat the remaining oil in a large frying pan. When it sizzles, add the beef rolls. Fry until browned all over, then lift out with a slotted spoon and drain in a colander.

6 Season the tomato sauce to taste, then add the beef rolls and spoon the sauce over them. Continue to simmer gently for about 30 minutes, adding a little water as necessary to prevent the sauce from getting too thick.

7 Serve with vegetables or with pasta, if you like.

SERVES 4 TO 6

135ml/9 tbsp extra virgin olive oil
1 medium onion, finely chopped
1 large celery stick, with leaves
   if possible, chopped
1 large carrot, finely chopped
500g/1¼lb fresh tomatoes, peeled
   and chopped, drained canned
   tomatoes or passata (bottled
   strained tomatoes)
8 thin slices of lean beef, such as
   minute steak
8 slices prosciutto crudo
45ml/3 tbsp finely chopped fresh
   flat leaf parsley
75ml/5 tbsp grated Pecorino cheese
sea salt and ground black pepper

PER PORTION Energy 324kcal/1346kJ; Protein 19.7g; Carbohydrate 5g, of which sugars 4.6g; Fat 25.2g, of which saturates 6.6g; Cholesterol 51mg; Calcium 184mg; Fibre 1.8g; Sodium 574mg.

SERVES 4

juice of l lemon
2 artichokes
50g/2oz prosciutto crudo,
   finely chopped
75g/3oz/6 tbsp butter, softened
8 thin slices of veal or beef,
   total weight 400g/14oz
45ml/3 tbsp plain (all-purpose) flour
30ml/2 tbsp vegetable oil
1 onion, thinly sliced
sea salt and ground black pepper

COOK'S TIP

If you place the meat slices
between sheets of clear film
(plastic wrap) before flattening
them, they will be less likely
to tear.

PER PORTION Energy 420kcal/1744kJ; Protein 26.3g;
Carbohydrate 10.1g, of which sugars 1.1g; Fat 30.7g,
of which saturates 14.9g; Cholesterol 108mg;
Calcium 28mg; Fibre 0.6g; Sodium 356mg.

BEEF ROLLS WITH ARTICHOKES
INVOLTINI CON CARCIOFI

This recipe has something very French about it, and was probably introduced by one
of the French chefs employed by the Sicilian aristocracy during the early 20th century.
It was de rigueur for every noble household to have a French chef or a monsù (an
Italian corruption of Monsieur) and the influence on Sicilian cooking is still evident.

1 Fill a heatproof bowl with boiling water and
add the lemon juice. Clean the artichokes and
trim them thoroughly, removing all the sharp
points and hard leaves. Drop them carefully
into the bowl of acidulated water and leave to
soak for about 10 minutes.

2 Meanwhile, put the chopped prosciutto in a
bowl and add half the butter. Stir until the
mixture forms a rough paste.

3 Lift the artichokes out of the water and stand
them upside down on a board to drain.
When they are cold, cut them into quarters and
remove the choke from each section. Cut each
quarter in half again to give 16 segments.

4 Flatten the meat slices by beating them with
a meat mallet or rolling pin until they are as
thin and flat as possible.

5 Spread a slice of meat with an eighth of the
butter and prosciutto mixture and lay 2 pieces
of artichoke on top. Season, roll up neatly and
tie with kitchen string (twine). Make seven more
in the same way, then coat all the rolls in flour.

6 Heat the remaining butter with the oil in a
large frying pan. Add the onion and fry for
5 minutes until softened but not browned.

7 Push the onion to one side and add the meat
rolls to the pan. Brown them over a medium
to high heat, then lower the heat and mix the
onions with the meat rolls.

8 Reduce the heat to the lowest setting, cover
the pan and simmer slowly, basting occasionally
with the juices in the pan, for 20 minutes or
until the meat is tender. Arrange on a heated
platter and serve.

GENZANO BAKED LAMB
AGNELLO ALLA GENZANESE

Genzano di Lucania is a town and commune in the province of Potenza, in the southern region of Basilicata. The citizens of this small town are called Genzanesi, which explains the name of this interesting, and very hearty, lamb dish. You can use any cut of lamb, as long as it is not too fatty and has been boned as much as possible.

1 Preheat the oven to 180°C/350°F/Gas 4. Put the breadcrumbs into a bowl and mix in the oregano, 2.5ml/½ tsp sea salt, parsley and garlic, using your hands.

2 Drizzle over half the olive oil and mix gently until the breadcrumbs stick together to form a mixture that resembles a crumble topping.

3 Peel the potatoes and slice them thickly and evenly. Use a little of the remaining oil to grease a baking dish that will hold all the meat and potatoes snugly.

4 Spread out the potatoes in an even layer on the base of the prepared baking dish, then drizzle with a little oil. Lay the lamb chunks evenly over the top.

5 Top with the breadcrumb mixture, then sprinkle over the remaining oil. Season lightly with salt. Drizzle over a little water to moisten.

6 Cover the dish with foil or baking parchment and bake for 1¼–1½ hours, until the meat and potatoes are tender and the topping is golden brown and crisp. Serve immediately.

SERVES 8

250g/8oz/5 cups soft
   white breadcrumbs
10ml/2 tsp dried oregano
60ml/4 tbsp finely chopped fresh
   flat leaf parsley
4 garlic cloves, finely chopped
250ml/8fl oz/1 cup extra virgin
   olive oil
2kg/4½lb yellow fleshed potatoes
2kg/4½lb lamb (any cut), boned
   and cut into chunks
sea salt

COOK'S TIP

If the topping has not browned sufficiently, remove the foil or paper and place the dish under a hot grill (broiler) for a few minutes.

PER PORTION Energy 932kcal/3904kJ; Protein 57.1g; Carbohydrate 64.6g, of which sugars 4.2g; Fat 51.3g, of which saturates 16.3g; Cholesterol 190mg; Calcium 88mg; Fibre 3.5g; Sodium 482mg.

SERVES 4 TO 6

1kg/2¼lb lamb, any cut, cut into
 big chunks
1 head of celery, roughly chopped
115g/4oz soft Pecorino cheese,
 cut into small pieces
150g/5oz small tomatoes,
 lightly crushed
1 large onion, sliced
7–8 dried bay leaves
a small handful of fresh flat leaf
 parsley, chopped
1 dried hot red chilli, chopped
sea salt

VARIATION

The taste of bay leaves is
very prominent and it is
traditionally intended to be so
in this dish. For a less pungent
flavour, use fewer leaves.

PER PORTION Energy 397kcal/1657kJ; Protein 40.9g;
Carbohydrate 1.9g, of which sugars 1.7g; Fat 25.2g,
of which saturates 12.6g; Cholesterol 146mg;
Calcium 271mg; Fibre 1g; Sodium 368mg.

PUGLIA LAMB CASSEROLE
CUTTURIEDDE

This is one of the oldest recipes still current in southern Italy, and comes from
Puglia, an area famous for its sheep trails. These run the length of the region,
from the Abruzzi to Lecce. The container in which the lamb is cooked is quite
important if you want the dish to be really authentic. In Puglia they traditionally
use a deep, copper pot with a narrow mouth to retain maximum flavour, but any
deep casserole that you have will work well.

1 Preheat the oven to 160°C/320°F/Gas 3.
Rinse and dry the chunks of lamb, checking
for any shards of bone.

2 Put the lamb in a big bowl and add the celery,
cheese, tomatoes, onion slices, herbs and chilli.
Season with salt. Mix well using clean hands.

3 Pack the mixture tightly into a casserole.
Cover with a sheet of baking parchment and
a heavy, tight-fitting lid.

4 Bake in the oven for about 3 hours, or until
the lamb is so tender that it has begun to fall
apart. Serve with roast potatoes, if you like.

POULTRY, MEAT AND GAME **89**

CALABRIAN RABBIT AND RED PEPPER STEW
CONIGLIO AI PEPERONI ALLA CALABRESE

This simple rabbit recipe comes from the region of Calabria, the 'toe' of Italy's famous boot shape. It is a long, slow-cooked dish flavoured with rich red wine and deliciously sweet red peppers. In Calabria the rabbit used would probably be wild as they are readily available in this region as throughout the rest of Italy, and therefore the meat would be quite gamey in flavour. Farmed rabbit, on the other hand, has a much milder taste. You can use either.

1 Clean the rabbit carefully, rinse it and pat the pieces dry with kitchen paper.

2 Place the rabbit pieces in a deep bowl, then add the bay leaves, celery, parsley, oregano, basil leaves and peppercorns.

3 Pour over the wine, cover the bowl and leave to stand for 2–3 hours at cool room temperature, or overnight in the refrigerator.

4 Using a slotted spoon, lift the pieces of rabbit out of the marinade and put them in a colander. Drain for 30 minutes, reserving the marinade.

5 Halve the peppers, remove the seeds and cut the flesh into large square pieces.

6 Heat the oil in a flameproof casserole. Add the onion and garlic and fry for 2 minutes.

7 Add the rabbit and fry, turning the pieces of rabbit occasionally, for 6–8 minutes, until the rabbit and onion have browned.

8 Pour in the marinade and add the peppers. Season with salt, stir, then cover tightly.

9 Simmer over a very low heat for about 50 minutes, or until the rabbit starts to fall off the bone and the peppers have cooked down to a thin purée. Serve in heated bowls.

SERVES 4

1 large rabbit, jointed
2 bay leaves
3 celery sticks, chopped
a handful of fresh parsley, chopped
5ml/1 tsp dried oregano
a handful of fresh basil leaves,
   lightly bruised
10 crushed peppercorns
350ml/12fl oz/1½ cups red wine
4 red (bell) peppers
90ml/6 tbsp olive oil
1 onion, thinly sliced
1 garlic clove, sliced
sea salt

> **COOK'S TIP**
>
> If the casserole is a bit watery at the end of the cooking time, remove the pieces of rabbit, raise the heat under the pan and boil the sauce, uncovered, until reduced and thickened. Return the rabbit to the pan and serve.

PER PORTION Energy 465kcal/1934kJ; Protein 31.8g; Carbohydrate 12.9g, of which sugars 12.1g; Fat 25.6g, of which saturates 5.9g; Cholesterol 147mg; Calcium 49mg; Fibre 3.4g; Sodium 68mg.

EGGS, VEGETABLES AND CHEESE
UOVA, VERDURE E FORMAGGIO

In Sicily, vegetables are not reserved for side dishes
and vegetarians, but are celebrated in a profusion of
recipes. Meaty aubergines, beautiful artichokes,
sweet peppers, juicy tomatoes and fresh courgettes
are just a few of the vegetables that are grown in
the sun-drenched south. As each vegetable comes
into season, it is lovingly and respectfully
transformed into a whole host of dishes. Spicy red
chillies are used in Calabria and Basilicata to give
the famous local heat to many recipes. Fresh eggs
are perfect for making an inexpensive and nutritious
meal, combined with fresh vegetables or spicy
chillies to make wonderful frittatas. Although it is
not used as copiously as in the north, cheese also
plays an important part in the southern Italian diet,
especially cheese made from sheep's milk.

CACIOCAVALLO, CHILLIES AND SAVOURY CAKES

In this dry and arid area of Italy, where rain is scarce, there is a shortage of lush green grass to support herds of cattle, so cheeses tend to be made from sheep's milk or a mixture of sheep's and cow's milk. These include Caciocavallo, originally produced in Sicily, but now spread all across Italy, which has an EU protected designation of origin status. It is shaped like a tear-drop and is similar in taste to the aged southern Italian Provolone cheese, with a hard edible rind. The Caciocavallo Silano is a different version, made with cow's milk in designated areas of southern Italy. Countless varieties of Pecorino, a basic sheep's milk cheese, exist in these regions and can be eaten when new and soft or aged and hard. Pecorino Siciliano is one of the oldest cheeses produced in Italy, and was recognized with a designation of origin in 1955. Also widely used is sheep's milk ricotta, which is popular as a fresh cheese as well as the matured, hard version that is used for grating.

The aubergine is the main vegetable of choice and there seems to be no end to the list of fantastic recipes using this versatile vegetable. There appears to be an innate respect for the vegetable, a timeless knowledge about how to use each variety to its best advantage and how to preserve them for the winter once the last crop of the summer has finished. The same reverence is reserved for the enormous, fleshy, sweet, misshapen peppers of Calabria, which are perfect when gently stewed in olive oil and wine with the deep purple onions of Tropea. Basilicata celebrates the dried red chilli, which is certainly one of the most important ingredients of the region, adding fiery flavour to many a dish.

CHILLI FRITTATA
FRITTATA COL PEPERONCINO

The Italian flat omelette, known as a frittata, can be made with all sorts of fillings, from cooked vegetables to leftover pasta. In Basilicata, spicy red chillies are often included, with the addition of Pecorino cheese for extra piquancy. Chillies are used liberally in the cooking of this region and are somewhat revered by the locals – a custom that dates from the times when it was believed that they offered protection from epidemic diseases such as the plague and cholera.

1 Heat the olive oil in a wide frying pan. Add the sliced hot chilli and fry over medium heat for 3 minutes. Strain into a large bowl, discarding the chilli and any seeds, and leave the chilli-flavoured oil to cool. Do not wipe the pan clean.

2 Break the eggs into the bowl with the chilli oil. Whisk lightly, then add the chopped red chilli and the Pecorino cheese. Beat well. Season with salt if necessary, but check first as Pecorino can be salty.

3 Reheat the frying pan, adding a little more olive oil if needed. When it is very hot, pour in the egg mixture. Shiver the pan so the mixture spreads evenly to the edges.

4 Cook for about 5 minutes over medium heat, occasionally lifting the edges of the frittata and tilting the pan so that liquid mixture flows underneath and sets. Do not let the base of the frittata burn.

5 Invert the frittata on to a large plate. The easiest way to do this is to place a large plate upside down on top of the frittata, covering it completely. Then, holding plate and pan firmly together, quickly turn both over. Slide the frittata back into the pan.

6 Return the pan to the heat and cook the frittata for a further 2–3 minutes, until the base is golden brown. Slide out on to a clean, flat platter and serve hot or cold.

SERVES 4

45ml/3 tbsp olive oil, plus extra
  if needed
1 very hot dried red chilli,
  sliced into rounds
5 eggs
1 medium hot dried red chilli,
  finely chopped
75g/3oz/¾ cup grated
  Pecorino cheese
sea salt (optional)

> **COOK'S TIPS**
>
> • As making a frittata is a skill that takes a little practice, you could start by making individual ones, using a small frying pan to make turning it easier.
> • If the frittata sticks to the pan, slide a palette knife or slim spatula underneath to free it before inverting it on the plate.

PER PORTION Energy 251kcal/1040kJ; Protein 15.2g; Carbohydrate 0g, of which sugars 0g; Fat 21.3g, of which saturates 6.9g; Cholesterol 257mg; Calcium 261mg; Fibre 0g; Sodium 292mg.

SERVES 4

500g/1¼lb large potatoes
1 slice cooked ham, about 25g/1oz
25g/1oz/1 cup fresh parsley leaves
25g/1oz/¼ cup coarsely grated
   Caciocavallo or Provolone cheese
2 eggs, separated
25g/1oz/¼ cup freshly grated
   Pecorino cheese
25g/1oz/2 tbsp unsalted butter
25g/1oz/¼ cup plain
   (all-purpose) flour
60ml/4 tbsp stale white breadcrumbs
sunflower oil for deep-frying
sea salt and ground black pepper

COOK'S TIP

Use a skewer to check that
the potatoes are tender.
To produce really fine and
creamy mashed potatoes, put
the cooked potatoes through
a food mill or ricer.

PER PORTION Energy 468kcal/1953kJ; Protein 15.4g;
Carbohydrate 37.6g, of which sugars 2.4g; Fat 29.5g,
of which saturates 9.2g; Cholesterol 126mg;
Calcium 216mg; Fibre 2.1g; Sodium 461mg.

SICILIAN FRIED POTATO ROLLS
CAZZILLI

These traditional croquettes are popular all over Sicily, and can be bought, piping
hot and crisp, from markets. When times were hard, meat was a luxury afforded
only by the few, so vegetables, which could be grown with relative ease, were often
combined with basic ingredients to create main course dishes to feed the family.

1 Put the unpeeled potatoes in a pan of salted
water and bring to the boil. Lower the heat,
cover the pan and simmer for 30 minutes.

2 Meanwhile, chop the ham and the parsley
together and set the mixture aside.

3 When the potatoes are tender, drain them,
peel them and mash them as finely as possible.

4 Scrape the mash into a bowl and stir in
the ham and parsley. Add the cheeses, egg
yolks and butter. Mix well, season with salt
and pepper and leave to cool. Lightly beat
the egg whites.

5 Put the flour, lightly beaten egg whites and
breadcrumbs in three separate shallow bowls.

6 Mould the potato mixture into sausage
shapes by rolling spoonfuls between the
palms of your hands. Coat them in flour, then
in egg white and finally in breadcrumbs.

7 Heat the oil for deep-frying until a small
piece of bread dropped into it sizzles instantly.
Add the cazzilli, in batches, and fry them for
2–3 minutes until crisp and golden all over.

8 Drain the cazzilli carefully on kitchen paper
and serve piping hot.

SAVOURY ARTICHOKE CAKE
TORTIERA DI CARCIOFI

This lovely artichoke recipe comes from Calabria. Artichokes have been cultivated in Sicily since the time of the Greeks, who called them kaktos. It is thought that they were introduced to France, along with other Italian ingredients, by Catherine de' Medici. It is recorded in the journal of Pierre de L'Estoile on June 19, 1576, that at the wedding of two courtiers, Queen Catherine de' Medici "ate so much that she thought she would die, and was very ill.... They said it was from eating too many artichoke bottoms". This is delicious served warm with a selection of salads.

1 Before preparing the artichokes, fill a bowl with water and add the lemon juice. Remove the hard, outer leaves from the artichokes and cut off the stalks. Snip off the sharp tips with a pair of scissors. Halve the artichokes and cut out and discard the furry chokes. Rub all the pieces of artichoke with the cut lemon to prevent discoloration. Slice in half again, then slice each quarter into three segments. Drop the pieces of artichoke into the acidulated water and leave to soak for 30 minutes.

2 Preheat the oven to 160°C/325°F/Gas 3. Use a little of the olive oil to generously grease a 20cm/8in cake tin (pan) that is at least 2cm/¾in deep. Add a quarter of the breadcrumbs to the tin. Turn and shake the tin to coat the sides and base with the crumbs.

3 Put the remaining breadcrumbs in a bowl and add the garlic, parsley and Pecorino cheese. Add a pinch of salt and about 15ml/1 tbsp of the olive oil.

4 Peel the potatoes and cut them in 2cm/¾in slices. Arrange a layer of potato slices on the base of the cake tin, taking care not to disturb the crumb lining.

5 Sprinkle some of the capers and a little of the herb-and-cheese-flavoured breadcrumbs over the potatoes.

6 Drain and dry the artichokes and arrange a layer of them over the breadcrumb mixture. Drizzle with olive oil. Repeat these layers until all the ingredients have been used, saving some oil to drizzle over the top. Press down to compress the layers.

7 Fit a flat lid or heavy ovenproof plate inside the cake tin to keep the layers compressed. Bake for 50 minutes.

8 Turn the cake tin carefully upside down so that the lid or plate is underneath. Stand it in a roasting pan. Reduce the oven to 140°C/275°F/Gas 1. Bake for a further 30 minutes.

9 Remove the cake tin from the oven and leave it to stand for 10 minutes before inverting the cake on a platter. Serve warm or at room temperature.

SERVES 4

6 large artichokes
juice of ½ lemon
1 lemon, cut in half
120ml/8 tbsp olive oil
45ml/3 tbsp soft white breadcrumbs
2 garlic cloves, very finely chopped
45ml/3 tbsp chopped fresh parsley
50g/2oz/½ cup freshly grated
    Pecorino cheese
4 medium to large potatoes
50g/2oz/⅓ cup capers, rinsed and
    roughly chopped
sea salt

> **COOK'S TIP**
> ....
> This savoury cake is delicious served just warm, accompanied by a selection of salads, such as a simple green salad and a tomato and red onion salad.

PER PORTION Energy 441kcal/1847kJ; Protein 10.6g; Carbohydrate 49.1g, of which sugars 3.7g; Fat 23.8g, of which saturates 5.5g; Cholesterol 13mg; Calcium 185mg; Fibre 2.9g; Sodium 257mg.

2 large aubergines (eggplants)
2 large tomatoes
300ml/½ pint/1¼ cups extra
    virgin olive oil
3 large onions, sliced into thin rings
2 large yellow (bell) peppers, cored,
    seeded and cut in thick strips
a handful of fresh parsley
a handful of fresh basil leaves
2 garlic cloves, peeled
about 10 thin slices of ciabatta,
    lightly toasted
sea salt and ground black pepper

LUCANIAN VEGETABLE CASSEROLE
PIATTO DI VERDURE ALLA LUCANA

Lucania is the old name for Basilicata. The name is said to derive from the Latin
'lucus non lucendo' (a dark grove with no light), since the area was covered with
dense forests. Many regional recipes, customs and traditions are still referred to as
Lucanian, including this ancient recipe for a deliciously fragrant vegetable casserole.

1 Cut the aubergines into cubes. Spread the
cubes out in a colander and sprinkle them
generously with salt. Stand the colander in
the sink. Fit a plate over the aubergines, put
a weight on top and leave them to drain for
about 1 hour.

2 Meanwhile, blanch the tomatoes. Cut a
cross in the base of each, put them in a
heatproof bowl and pour over boiling water
to cover. Leave for 1–2 minutes or until the
skin starts to peel back from the crosses.

3 Drain the tomatoes, peel them, cut them
into cubes and discard the seeds.

4 Heat the oil in a large, shallow pan. Add the
onions and fry for 3–4 minutes until softened
but not browned.

5 Rinse the aubergine cubes, pat them dry with
kitchen paper, then add them to the onions.
Cook, stirring frequently, for 5 minutes, then
stir in the peppers and tomatoes. Season with
salt and pepper and simmer for 10 minutes.

6 Chop the parsley and basil with the garlic.
Add the mixture to the pan and stir to mix.
Cook, uncovered, for about 45 minutes, until
the mixture is thick and flavoursome. Serve
hot or cold with slices of toasted ciabatta.

PER PORTION Energy 961kcal/4012kJ; Protein 19.5g;
Carbohydrate 98.1g, of which sugars 21.3g;
Fat 57.2g, of which saturates 8.1g; Cholesterol 0mg;
Calcium 261mg; Fibre 10.2g; Sodium 826mg.

BAKED AUBERGINES WITH MOZZARELLA
MELANZANE AL FORNO CON MOZZARELLA

In various parts of Europe, eating aubergines was once alleged to cause madness, leprosy, cancer and bad breath, and these superstitions led to its being used largely as a decorative plant. It wasn't until the 18th century that aubergines were established as a food in Italy and France. Sicilians love aubergines as this delicious dish shows.

1 Slice the aubergines into 2cm/¾in rounds. Spread them out in a colander and sprinkle generously with salt. Stand the colander in the sink, fit a plate inside to cover the aubergines, put a weight on top and drain for 1–2 hours.

2 Meanwhile, put the eggs in a bowl. Season with salt and pepper and beat them lightly.

3 Rinse the aubergines to remove the excess salt, drain well, then pat dry with kitchen paper. Coat the slices lightly in flour.

4 Heat the oil in a large frying pan. When it sizzles, add the floured aubergine slices, in batches if necessary, and fry for about 3 minutes on each side, until crisp and golden.

5 Remove the aubergines from the frying pan with a slotted spoon and allow to drain on kitchen paper.

6 Preheat the oven to 200°C/400°F/Gas 6. Arrange half the aubergine slices in a roasting pan. Top each one with a slice of mozzarella and a few pieces of anchovy.

7 Cover with the remaining fried aubergine slices to form small sandwiches. Press the sandwiches tightly together to prevent them from falling apart.

8 Season with a little salt, sprinkle evenly with the breadcrumbs and bake for 10 minutes. Serve immediately.

SERVES 4 TO 6

500g/1¼lb aubergines (eggplants)
2 eggs
plain (all-purpose) white flour
350ml/12fl oz/1½ cups olive oil
150g/5oz mozzarella cheese, thinly sliced
4 salted anchovies, washed and boned, then chopped finely
60ml/4 tbsp stale white breadcrumbs
sea salt and ground black pepper

PER PORTION Energy 458kcal/1897kJ; Protein 10.3g; Carbohydrate 10.9g, of which sugars 2g; Fat 41.9g, of which saturates 8.7g; Cholesterol 78mg; Calcium 141mg; Fibre 1.9g; Sodium 429mg.

STUFFED BAKED PEPPERS PUGLIESE-STYLE
PEPERONI RIPIENI ALLA PUGLIESE

Served with a salad, this makes a wonderful vegetarian main course or antipasto dish. The countryside of Puglia is incredibly fertile, producing abundant grain, tomatoes, grapes, artichokes, lettuces, fennel, peppers and onions, as well as fine olive oil. Local cooks have a simple dictum which translates as, "There's no need to complicate things: just combine the best local ingredients and delicious dishes will practically create themselves."

1 Using a sharp knife, slice the top off each pepper to form a lid. Set the lids aside. Keeping the peppers intact, carefully remove the core and seeds from each. Rinse out the cavities, then stand the peppers upside down on kitchen paper to drain.

2 Peel the potatoes and cut them into large cubes. Bring a pan of lightly salted water to the boil, add the potato cubes and parboil them for 5 minutes. Drain.

3 Preheat the oven to 180°C/350°F/Gas 4. Oil a deep baking dish that is large enough to hold the four peppers comfortably.

4 Put the potatoes into the dish and level the surface. Dot with the cherry tomatoes, then sprinkle over the onion slices, and half the garlic and parsley.

5 Top with half the Pecorino and season with salt and pepper. Moisten with a little water and drizzle with about half the oil.

6 Put the eggs in a bowl. Add the breadcrumbs, then add the remaining Pecorino cheese, as well as the remaining parsley and garlic. Stir in the Parmesan cheese. Season with salt and pepper. Mix well, then stir in half the remaining olive oil.

7 Using a spoon, fill the hollow peppers three-quarters full with the egg and breadcrumb mixture, then replace the lids.

8 Stand the peppers upright on the bed of vegetables in the baking dish. Use the potato cubes as wedges, if necessary, to prevent the stuffed peppers from falling over.

9 Season with salt and pepper, drizzle over the remaining olive oil and bake the peppers for 1 hour, stirring the vegetable mixture gently from time to time. Cover the baking dish loosely with foil if the top seems to be browning too much during cooking. Take care not to overbalance the peppers. This dish can be served hot or cold.

SERVES 4

4 large yellow (bell) peppers
800g/1¾lb potatoes
200ml/7fl oz/scant 1 cup extra virgin olive oil, plus extra for greasing
8 cherry tomatoes, sliced in half
1 large onion, sliced
2 garlic cloves, sliced
2 large fresh flat leaf parsley sprigs, roughly chopped
75g/3oz/¾ cup freshly grated Pecorino cheese
3 eggs
40g/1½oz/¾ cup fresh white breadcrumbs
40g/1½oz/½ cup grated Parmesan cheese
sea salt and ground black pepper

COOK'S TIP

If the vegetables seem to dry out too much during cooking, pour a little water into the base of the baking dish to keep them moist.

PER PORTION Energy 716kcal/2982kJ; Protein 22.8g; Carbohydrate 52g, of which sugars 14.3g; Fat 47.7g, of which saturates 12g; Cholesterol 171mg; Calcium 432mg; Fibre 5.8g; Sodium 477mg.

YELLOW PUMPKIN WITH MINT AND CAPERS
ZUCCA GIALLA ALLA CALABRESE

This vegetable dish is almost a salad, and is good served with cold meats, especially roast beef. Pumpkins originated in Central America and would have found their way to Italy along with tomatoes, potatoes and tobacco, with New World explorers. This recipe calls for the yellow-fleshed pumpkin that holds its shape when fried.

1 Cut the pumpkin into neat, even slices. Spread these out in a colander and sprinkle with salt. Cover with a plate, put a weight on top and stand the colander in the sink. Leave it to drain for 1 hour.

2 Rinse the pumpkin to remove the excess salt. Drain well, then pat the pieces dry with kitchen paper.

3 Heat the sunflower oil in a wide pan until a small piece of bread, dropped into the oil, sizzles instantly.

4 Fry the pumpkin slices, in batches, for about 4 minutes on each side, then lift them out with a slotted spoon and drain on kitchen paper.

5 In a bowl, mix together the olive oil, vinegar, capers, garlic, mint and half the breadcrumbs.

6 Spread out half the fried pumpkin slices in a shallow dish and spoon over half the dressing. Cover with the rest of the pumpkin, then the remaining dressing. Press down firmly and coat with the remaining breadcrumbs. Leave to stand for 1 hour before serving.

SERVES 4 TO 6

800g/1¾lb yellow pumpkin, peeled
  and seeded
60ml/4 tbsp coarse salt
sunflower oil for deep-frying
150ml/¼ pint/⅔ cup olive oil
60ml/4 tbsp red wine vinegar
45ml/3 tbsp salted capers, rinsed
  and finely chopped
5 garlic cloves, very thinly sliced
75ml/5 tbsp chopped fresh mint
120ml/8 tbsp fresh white
  breadcrumbs

COOK'S TIP

The red wine vinegar should be really strongly flavoured. This will give the dish plenty of sharpness, which cuts the sweetness of the pumpkin.

PER PORTION Energy 373kcal/1545kJ; Protein 3.5g; Carbohydrate 18.7g, of which sugars 3g; Fat 32.1g, of which saturates 4.2g; Cholesterol 0mg; Calcium 81mg; Fibre 2.2g; Sodium 155mg.

SERVES 4 TO 6

8 medium courgettes
   (zucchini), trimmed
250ml/8fl oz/1 cup olive oil
12 fresh mint leaves,
   roughly chopped
150ml/¼ pint/⅔ cup light red
   wine vinegar
2 large garlic cloves, chopped
sea salt

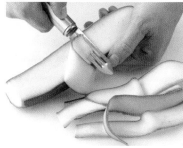

COOK'S TIP

This delicate and pretty dish will look even more attractive if you use a mixture of both yellow and green courgettes (zucchini).

PER PORTION Energy 244kcal/1004kJ; Protein 1.9g; Carbohydrate 1.9g, of which sugars 1.8g; Fat 25.4g, of which saturates 3.6g; Cholesterol 0mg; Calcium 33mg; Fibre 1.1g; Sodium 2mg.

POOR WOMAN'S COURGETTES
ZUCCHINE ALLA POVERELLA

This traditional way of preparing courgettes comes from Basilicata, and gets its name from the fact that all its ingredients are cheap and readily available. Most people who cultivate their own courgettes will also have garlic and mint growing in the garden, and oil and vinegar in the kitchen.

1 Using a potato peeler, slice the courgettes lengthways into thin strips.

2 Heat the oil in a shallow pan. When it is very hot, add the courgette strips, in batches, and fry for about 4 minutes on each side or until softened and golden.

3 Lift out the courgettes with a slotted spoon and drain on kitchen paper.

4 Layer the courgettes in a heatproof dish, sprinkling each layer with a little salt and chopped mint. Set aside.

5 Pour the wine vinegar into a pan and add a pinch of salt. Stir in the garlic and the remaining mint. Bring to the boil. Cook for 5 minutes, then pour the hot marinade all over the courgettes. Leave to stand until cold, then cover and place in the refrigerator. Serve lightly chilled.

1 head of white celery, separated
  into sticks, leaves reserved
45ml/3 tbsp olive oil
3 garlic cloves, chopped
1 onion, chopped
2 x 400g/14oz cans plum tomatoes,
  drained and sieved (strained)
sea salt and ground black pepper

CELERY IN TOMATO SAUCE
COSTE AL SUGO

Celery and onion, which, along with carrot, are the constituents of the French mirepoix,
are equally popular in Italian cooking. They form the background flavouring for many
savoury dishes. Stocks, stews, soups and sauces almost always contain celery, and in
the south the leaves are often added for extra flavour, much as a herb might be.

1 Using a sharp knife, trim the celery sticks,
removing any tough strings. Cut into chunks
and place in a bowl. Chop the leaves finely and
set them aside in a separate bowl.

2 Heat the olive oil in a wide pan and add the
garlic and onion. Cook for 3–4 minutes, until
the onion has softened but not browned.

3 Stir in the celery chunks. Cook for 5 minutes.

4 Pour in the tomatoes, stir and season to
taste. Cover the pan and simmer the mixture
for about 15 minutes or until the celery is soft.

5 Stir in the chopped celery leaves, spoon the
mixture into a heated dish and serve.

COOK'S TIP

Stringing the celery stalks is
important, as the strings will
not break down during the
cooking process and if left,
would spoil the dish.

PER PORTION Energy 115kcal/480kJ; Protein 1.7g;
Carbohydrate 7.6g, of which sugars 7.2g; Fat 8.9g,
of which saturates 1.4g; Cholesterol 0mg;
Calcium 26mg; Fibre 2.4g; Sodium 31mg.

SPINACH SALAD WITH BASIL
INSALATA DI SPINACI E BASIL

This deliciously crunchy and refreshing green salad from Basilicata owes its pungent flavour to fresh basil. The herb grows best in hot, dry conditions, so is very well suited to the climate of southern Italy.

1 Remove and discard the stalks from the spinach, then wash the leaves and dry them thoroughly. Place them in a salad bowl and add the chopped peppers, sliced onion and basil leaves.

2 Pour the lemon juice into a separate bowl. Whisk in the oil. Season with salt and pepper.

3 Pour the dressing over the salad, toss thoroughly and serve at once.

SERVES 6

450g/1lb fresh spinach leaves
2 small green (bell) peppers, halved,
  seeded and roughly chopped
1 onion, thinly sliced
about 8 fresh basil leaves
20ml/4 tsp lemon juice
60ml/4 tbsp extra virgin olive oil
sea salt and ground black pepper

COOK'S TIP

This salad should be fresh and crisp so dress the salad only a few minutes before serving. If you dress it in advance the leaves will wilt.

PER PORTION Energy 107kcal/443kJ; Protein 2.8g; Carbohydrate 6g, of which sugars 5g; Fat 8.1g, of which saturates 1.1g; Cholesterol 0mg; Calcium 139mg; Fibre 2.6g; Sodium 107mg.

DESSERTS AND BAKING
DOLCI

The art of opulent pastries and over-the-top ice-cream creations comes into its own in a Sicilian pastry shop or gelateria. While home-baking and dessert-making remains quite simple and low key, there is no shortage of choice in the pasticcerie of even the smallest provincial town. At the seaside resort of San Leo, for example, on the western coast near Agrigento, the local gelateria, known as Le Cuspidi, offers more than 40 flavours of ice cream, each one more wildly exotic and imaginative than the last, and all of them delicious. The tradition of squashing a generous scoop or two of ice cream inside a soft brioche bun is about as Sicilian as can be, and is a wonderfully satisfying way to enjoy gelato at any time of day, even at breakfast, as many locals do during the hottest days of summer.

PASTRIES, CASSATA
AND FROZEN TREATS

All over Sicily, Calabria, Basilicata and Puglia, the almond is a vital ingredient for many simple home-made biscuits (cookies), often combined with other local products, such as dried figs, raisins, pine kernels and honey. Along with the widespread use of candied fruit, these ingredients form the basis for numerous recipes, many of which are linked with religious festivities. These festivities range from traditional Christian celebrations, such as Easter or Christmas, to obscure local saints' day celebrations, such as Saint Joseph's day, when sweet and sticky Honey-coated Fritters are eaten in Calabria.

There is a world of difference between the cakes and desserts that local cooks make at home and the complicated, intricate and often dramatic desserts on sale in local shops. Sicily is considered to be the best place in the whole country to enjoy ice cream, but the island is also proud of many other specialities that can be admired in the local pasticcerie. Among these is cassata, the emblematic dessert of the city of Palermo, with its thick, pale green icing hiding a sponge cake filled with more sweetened, flavoured icing (confectioners') sugar and candied fruit.

Modica, in Sicily, is a town made famous for a special kind of chocolate that is prepared according to a traditional recipe dating back to the ancient Aztec civilization, which was handed down by the Spaniards who controlled Sicily from the 13th to 15th centuries.

Sweetmeats exist in varying forms throughout the southern regions, such as cuccidati in Sicily and petrali in Calabria, but all are rich and flavoursome and can be stored for months in the refrigerator with the occasional addition of some dessert wine.

HONEY-COATED FRITTERS
ZEPPOLE A VENTO

The ingredients for this very sticky, honey-coated Calabrian sweet could not be simpler, yet the skill of the local cooks transforms them into something that is pretty to look at and delicious to eat. Zeppole are traditionally made on La Festa di San Giuseppe (Saint Joseph's Day) on March 19. In Rome, Naples and Sicily, these little pastries are sometimes sold on street corners and are given away as gifts. In certain parts of Calabria, savoury anchovy zeppole are eaten on New Year's Eve and New Year's Day.

1 Pour the water into a heavy pan and bring it to the boil. Gradually trickle in the flour, stirring constantly. Continue to stir until the mixture forms a dough and comes away from the sides of the pan. Turn the dough into a bowl and leave to cool completely.

2 Pinch off small pieces of dough and roll them into small sausage shapes, each about 5cm/2in long and 5mm/¼in wide. Squeeze each sausage in the middle to make a bow shape.

3 Heat the oil in a large pan until a small piece of bread dropped into it sizzles instantly.

4 Add the dough shapes, in batches, and fry until they rise to the surface of the oil and turn golden and crisp.

5 As each batch cooks, lift the bows out with a slotted spoon and drain on kitchen paper. Place them on a warmed heatproof platter and keep them warm while cooking the remaining shapes.

6 Heat the honey in a small pan. When it bubbles, pour it all over the fritters.

7 Allow to cool slightly, then serve while warm.

MAKES ABOUT 30

500ml/17fl oz/generous 2 cups
    cold water
500g/1¼lb/5 cups very fine plain
    (all-purpose) white flour or cake
    flour, sifted twice
light olive oil for deep-frying
90ml/6 tbsp clear honey

> **COOK'S TIP**
>
> It is important to stir constantly while the flour mixture cooks, as this will prevent lumps from forming. The paste must be smooth. Serve the fritters with a dish of orange wedges, which will cut the intense sweetness of the honey.

PER FRITTER Energy 103kcal/431kJ; Protein 1.6g; Carbohydrate 13g, of which sugars 0.3g; Fat 5.3g, of which saturates 0.8g; Cholesterol 0mg; Calcium 23mg; Fibre 0.5g; Sodium 1mg.

MAKES ABOUT 25

250g/9oz/2¼ cups whole
   blanched almonds
250g/9oz/generous 1 cup sugar
75ml/5 tbsp cold water
350g/12oz/3 cups plain (all-purpose)
   white flour, sifted twice

COOK'S TIP

Keep a close eye on the
almonds while toasting them
in the oven, as they scorch
readily. They could also be
toasted under the grill (broiler)
or in a hot, dry pan, but since
the oven is required for
baking, it does make sense
to use it.

PER COOKIE Energy 148kcal/625kJ; Protein 3.5g;
Carbohydrate 22g, of which sugars 11.1g; Fat 5.8g,
of which saturates 0.5g; Cholesterol 0mg;
Calcium 49mg; Fibre 1.2g; Sodium 2mg.

PUGLIESE ALMOND COOKIES
MUSTAZZUELI

These simple almond cookies from Puglia seem incredibly hard when you first
attempt to bite into them, but once in your mouth they crumble very satisfactorily,
and can also be dunked in dessert wine. A similar style of biscuit or cookie is
made in the Cosenza area of Calabria, where they are known as mostaccioli.
The Calabrian recipe adds a little aniseed liqueur and some grated orange rind
to the mixture, and the resulting texture is lighter.

1 Preheat the oven to 200°C/400°F/Gas 6.
Scatter the almonds evenly over 1 or 2 baking
sheets and toast them in the oven for about
5 minutes, or until golden brown. Take the
almonds out of the oven, but leave the oven
switched on.

2 Put the sugar into a small pan. Add the
water and stir over a low heat until the sugar
has dissolved and the mixture has formed a
smooth syrup. Cool slightly.

3 Grind the almonds to a fine powder in a food
processor or nut mill. Put three-quarters of the
flour on to a clean work surface. Make a hollow
in the centre with your fist. Pour the ground
almonds into the hollow and add the syrup.

4 Mix the syrup into the flour and almonds
with your hands, working quickly to achieve
a smooth and elastic dough.

5 Scatter half the remaining flour on the work
surface. Shape the dough into a cylinder with
a diameter of about 4cm/1½in.

6 Using a sharp knife, cut the cylinder into
about 20 even discs, then flatten each one with
the palm of your hand, lightly floured, so that
you reduce its thickness to about 5mm/¼in.

7 Cut each disc into a roughly square shape
using a 4cm/1½in biscuit (cookie) cutter, and
re-shape the excess dough. Use the remaining
flour to dust one or more baking sheets.
Arrange the cookies in rows on the baking
sheet(s). Bake for 10–15 minutes, until golden.

8 Leave the cookies on the baking sheets for
1–2 minutes to firm up, then, using a spatula,
transfer them to wire racks to cool completely.
Stored in airtight containers, the mustazzueli
will keep for up to 1 month.

SICILIAN FIG PASTRIES
CUCCIDATI

The sticky, nutty, Sicilian sweetmeat that forms the centre of these pastries is also wonderful on its own or with salty Pecorino cheese. About one-tenth of the sweetmeat will be used to fill the pastries in this recipe, but there is no point making it in small batches as it keeps extremely well for up to a year, so store the rest in your refrigerator. The flavour develops and changes over the months, as the mixture ferments gently with the monthly addition of the dessert wine.

1 First make the sweetmeat. Put the figs and sultanas or raisins in a bowl with water to cover. Soak for 30 minutes. Drain the soaked fruit and transfer the mixture to a pan. Pour over fresh water to cover. Bring to simmering point and cook for 2–3 minutes to soften. Allow to cool.

2 Chop the walnuts and almonds finely in a food processor. Scrape into a bowl and set aside.

3 Drain the figs and sultanas and process them briefly in a food processor until chopped, but not puréed. With the motor running, add the honey and half the wine or sherry through the feeder tube. Process until mixed. Remove the lid from the food processor and add the grated lemon and orange rind to the mixture. Replace the lid and process until reasonably smooth.

4 Scrape the mixture into a large bowl, add the chopped nuts and mix well, adding more wine or sherry as needed. The consistency should be medium to dry.

5 Set aside 90–120ml/6–8 tbsp of the mixture and spoon the rest into a plastic container, close the lid securely and store in the refrigerator (see Cook's Tips).

6 Preheat the oven to 180°C/350°F/Gas 4. Grease 2 baking sheets. Put the butter in a bowl and beat it with a wooden spoon until creamed. Beat in the sugar, eggs or egg yolks, milk and vanilla extract, adding a little flour if the mixture shows signs of curdling.

7 Sift in the flour, baking powder and salt. Mix to a soft dough. Cover and chill for at least 1 hour.

8 Using a teaspoon, scoop up a little of the mixture. Roll into a ball and place on one of the baking sheets, then press the top to flatten it to a round. Repeat with the remaining mixture, leaving room for spreading. Spoon a little of the sweetmeat on to each round and pull up the edges to partially cover the filling.

9 Bake for 10 minutes or until golden. Leave on the baking sheets for 5 minutes, then transfer to wire racks and sprinkle with caster sugar. Leave to cool.

MAKES ABOUT 24

200g/7oz/scant 1 cup unsalted
  butter, softened
400g/14oz/2 cups caster (superfine)
  sugar, plus extra for sprinkling
2 eggs or 4 egg yolks, well beaten
30ml/2 tbsp milk
5ml/1 tsp vanilla extract
500g/1¼lb/4½ cups plain
  (all-purpose) white flour
10ml/2 tsp baking powder
3ml/½ tsp salt

FOR THE SWEETMEAT

450g/1lb/2⅔ cups hard dried figs
450g/1lb/2⅔ cups sultanas
  (golden raisins) or raisins
115g/4oz/1 cup shelled walnuts
115g/4oz/1 cup blanched almonds
500g/1¼lb/2 cups clear honey
300ml/½ pint/1¼ cups sweet
  dessert wine or sherry
finely grated rind of
  1 unwaxed lemon
finely grated rind of
  1 unwaxed orange

COOK'S TIPS
• If your food processor does not have a powerful motor, chop the nuts roughly with a knife before processing them.
• The sweetmeat will keep in the refrigerator for up to 1 year, provided about 5ml/1 tsp dessert wine or sherry is stirred in once a month to keep the mixture moist and lightly fermented.

PER PASTRY Energy 423kcal/1783kJ; Protein 5.5g; Carbohydrate 70g, of which sugars 54g; Fat 13.9g, of which saturates 5.2g; Cholesterol 35mg; Calcium 117mg; Fibre 2.9g; Sodium 90mg.

CALABRIAN PASTRIES
PETRALI

To make these traditional pastries, the filling must be left for 12 hours before baking to allow the flavours to develop. Versions of these simple yet extremely rich pastries are found all over Calabria. It is quite likely that they were originally created in convents, where the nuns would busy themselves by preparing vast quantities to sell to the locals. In some parts of the region they are a traditional Christmas treat, but petrali are also made to celebrate St Martin's Day in summer, when they are known as Pitte di San Martino.

MAKES ABOUT 20

500g/1lb/ 2½ cups plain
    (all-purpose) white flour
2 small (US medium) egg yolks
75g/2oz/¼ cup lard or white
    cooking fat (shortening), diced
100g/4oz/scant ½ cup sugar
scant 40ml/2½ tbsp sweet vermouth
3½ml/¾ tsp baking powder
7.5ml/1½ tsp olive oil

FOR THE FILLING
400g/14oz/2⅓ cups dried figs
400g/14oz/2⅓ cups whole
    blanched almonds
400g/14oz/2⅓ cups walnut halves
400g/14oz/1¾ cups clear honey
2.5ml/½ tsp ground cinnamon
2.5ml/½ tsp ground cloves
50ml/2fl oz/¼ cup sweet
    dessert wine

FOR THE ICING
135ml/9 tbsp icing
    (confectioners') sugar
multicoloured sugar
    strands (optional)

1 Start by making the filling. Cut the dried figs into quarters and put them in a pan. Slice the almonds in half and add them to the pan with the walnut halves, honey, spices and wine. Stir over a low heat for 10 minutes.

2 Remove the pan from the heat, cover and set aside for 12 hours.

3 To make the dough, put the flour on to a clean work top and make a hollow in the centre with your fist.

4 Put the egg yolks, lard or cooking fat, sugar, vermouth, baking powder and olive oil into the hollow. Mix these ingredients together, gradually incorporating the surrounding flour to make a dough.

5 Knead the dough until smooth and elastic, but do not overwork it. Cover with clear film (plastic wrap) and leave to rest for 30 minutes.

6 Roll out the dough on a lightly floured board to a thickness of 5mm/¼in. Using a 10–12cm/4–5in pastry cutter or upturned glass, cut it into rounds.

7 Spoon a little of the fig and nut mixture over one half of each round and fold over to make miniature pasties. Seal the edges carefully by pressing them together with the tines of a fork. Alternatively, top the round with the fruit and nut mixture, leaving the pastry rim clear, and cover with a pastry lattice.

8 Preheat the oven to 180°C/350°F/Gas 4. Arrange the petrali on lightly oiled baking sheets. Bake them for 10–15 minutes, until pale golden.

9 Transfer them on to wire racks to cool completely.

10 Sprinkle the petrali with icing sugar. Alternatively, mix the icing sugar with enough water to make a thick, spreadable paste and spread the icing over the petrali. If you like you could also sprinkle them with multicoloured sugar strands before the icing sets.

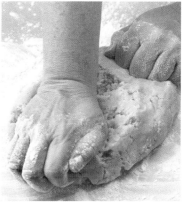

PER PASTRY Energy 541kcal/2267kJ; Protein 10.7g; Carbohydrate 60.1g, of which sugars 40.4g; Fat 30g, of which saturates 3.8g; Cholesterol 24mg; Calcium 162mg; Fibre 4.5g; Sodium 22mg.

SICILIAN CASSATA
LA CASSATA SICILIANA

This rich and sumptuous Sicilian classic is traditionally made in springtime. Its origins lie deep in Sicily's culinary history, and it takes its name from an Arab word meaning big round bowl. The dessert – not the ice cream version – used to be made and sold by the nuns of Palermo's convents. The story goes that the business became so successful, and the Holy Sisters so absorbed in making cassata, that they began to neglect their prayers and holy duties. Eventually they received an official reprimand from the Archbishop.

1 Press the ricotta cheese through a sieve (strainer) into a bowl. Gradually mix in the icing sugar until the mixture has the consistency of lightly whipped cream.

2 Flavour the ricotta mixture with the vanilla extract and rum or liqueur, then stir in the grated or shaved chocolate and the candied peel.

3 Line a 15cm/6in bowl with clear film (plastic wrap), making sure there is plenty of overhang. Line the base and sides of the bowl with slices of sponge or pound cake, using the custard to cement the slices together securely.

4 Fill with the ricotta mixture and level the top carefully. Bring the surplus film over the cassata to cover the surface. Put a plate on the top of the film, fitting it inside the bowl, press it down, then chill the dessert in the refrigerator for 2–3 hours.

5 Meanwhile, make the fondant icing. Dissolve the sugar in the water in a large, heavy pan over low heat. Wipe down the sides of the pan with a clean brush dipped in cold water to prevent crystals from forming.

6 Dissolve the cream of tartar in a little water, then stir into the syrup in the pan. Bring to the boil and boil steadily until the syrup registers 115°C/242°F on a sugar thermometer, or when a drop of icing forms a soft ball when dropped into a small bowl of cold water.

7 Slowly pour the syrup into a heatproof bowl and set aside until a skin forms on the surface. Beat it with a wooden spoon until opaque and firm. When cool enough to handle, knead it until smooth. Cover and set aside.

8 Remove the plate from the cassata, unfold the film and invert a plate on top. Turn plate and dessert over and lift off the bowl. Remove the film.

9 Ice the dessert with the fondant icing. Decorate it with chocolate flakes, candied fruit, glacé fruit, silver balls, sugared almonds, pistachio halves, coloured dragées and rice paper flowers. Chill until ready to serve.

SERVES 4

500g/1¼lb/2½ cups very fresh ricotta cheese
300g/11oz/scant 3 cups icing (confectioners') sugar, sifted
5ml/1 tsp vanilla extract
45ml/3 tbsp rum or liqueur
50g/2oz dark (bittersweet) chocolate, grated or shaved
50g/2oz/⅓ cup chopped mixed candied peel
300g/11oz sponge or pound cake, cut in thin slices
90ml/6 tbsp custard
chocolate flakes, candied and glacé fruit, silver balls, sugared almonds, pistachio halves, coloured dragées (candies) and rice paper flowers, to decorate

FOR THE FONDANT ICING
450g/1lb/2 cups caster (superfine) sugar
150ml/¼ pint/⅔ cup water
2.5ml/½ tsp cream of tartar

PER PORTION Energy 1078kcal/4564kJ; Protein 13.9g; Carbohydrate 211.6g, of which sugars 209.8g; Fat 22.8g, of which saturates 13.5g; Cholesterol 54mg; Calcium 134mg; Fibre 0g; Sodium 31mg.

REGGIO CALABRIA CAKE
TORTA REGGINA

This delectable dish resembles a classic fruit pie, although the sweet pastry is delightfully different from the usual pastry that encases fruit pies. It is a wonderful way to make the most of summer and autumn fruits, even when they are slightly past their best. The recipe comes from Reggio di Calabria, commonly known as Reggio, an ancient city that is over 2,700 years old. It is situated right on the toe of the Italian peninsula, just over the Strait of Messina from Sicily.

SERVES 6

1kg/2¼lb assorted fresh fruit such as apples, pears, cherries and plums
275g/10oz/2½ cups plain (all-purpose) white flour
2 egg yolks
200g/7oz/scant 1 cup unsalted butter, diced, plus softened butter for greasing
finely grated rind of 1 lemon
200g/7oz/scant 1 cup caster (superfine) sugar
1 beaten egg, for glazing

COOK'S TIP

On a hot day, it is better to rest the pastry in the refrigerator rather than at room temperature.

1 Peel and core or stone (pit) all the fruit. Slice and poach lightly in water until just tender. Drain very thoroughly and set aside.

2 Pile the flour on a clean work surface and make a hollow in the centre with your fist. Add the egg yolks, butter, lemon rind and half the sugar to the hollow.

3 Mix to a very soft pastry with your hands and knead gently. Wrap in clear film (plastic wrap) and set aside to rest for about 20 minutes.

4 Preheat the oven to 200°C/400°F/Gas 6. Grease a shallow 23cm/9in cake tin (pan) with butter.

5 Roll out half the pastry on a lightly floured surface and line the bottom and sides of the cake tin. Do not worry if the pastry breaks or cracks; just use your fingers to press it back together.

6 Check that the fruit is well drained, then spoon it into the lined tin. Sprinkle the remaining sugar over the top.

7 Roll out the remaining pastry and make a lid for the pie. Fit it over the fruit, pinch the pastry edges together to seal, and brush with beaten egg.

8 Bake for 40 minutes, until the pastry is golden and the filling is cooked. Serve cold.

PER PORTION Energy 612kcal/2571kJ; Protein 6.1g; Carbohydrate 85.3g, of which sugars 50.4g; Fat 29.8g, of which saturates 18.6g; Cholesterol 144mg; Calcium 101mg; Fibre 4.1g; Sodium 260mg.

CALABRIAN LEMON TART
CROSTATA ALLA CREMA DI LIMONE

Citrus fruits come into their own under the baking hot Calabrian sun. This deliciously tangy lemon tart uses lots of freshly grated lemon rind for a really intense flavour. Serve it cold with a small glass of Limoncello for a delicious grown-up dessert.

1 Put the plain flour in a bowl. Add the chopped butter and rub it in until the mixture resembles fine breadcrumbs.

2 Stir in the sugar and add the egg and egg yolk. Mix to a soft dough. Knead lightly, wrap in clear film (plastic wrap) and chill until required.

3 While the pastry is resting, make the filling. Heat the custard and stir in the sugar and lemon rind until the sugar is dissolved, then cover the surface of the custard with baking parchment and leave it to cool.

4 Preheat the oven to 180°C/350°F/Gas 4. Grease a 20cm/8in tart tin (pan) with butter. Beat the ricotta into the custard, then add the beaten egg. Mix thoroughly.

5 On a large sheet of baking parchment, roll out the pastry using a lightly floured rolling pin. Line the tart tin and trim the edges.

6 Pour the lemon filling into the tart case and bake in the oven for 30 minutes. Leave to cool, then dust with icing sugar. Serve at room temperature or cold.

SERVES 6

250g/9oz/2¼ cups plain
  (all-purpose) flour, plus extra
  for dusting
125g/4¼oz/generous ½ cup cold
  unsalted butter, chopped, plus
  softened butter for greasing
115g/4oz/½ cup caster
  (superfine) sugar
1 egg, plus 1 egg yolk
icing (confectioners') sugar,
  for dusting

FOR THE FILLING

250ml/8fl oz/generous
  1 cup custard
115g/4oz/½ cup sugar
250g/9oz/generous 1 cup
  ricotta cheese
1 egg, beaten
finely grated rind of
  3–4 unwaxed lemons

COOK'S TIP

When lining the tart tin (pan), do not stretch the pastry or it will shrink when baked.

PER PORTION Energy 605kcal/2539kJ; Protein 12.2g; Carbohydrate 80.5g, of which sugars 46.7g; Fat 28.3g, of which saturates 15.9g; Cholesterol 162mg; Calcium 149mg; Fibre 1.3g; Sodium 218mg.

750ml/1¼ pints/3 cups fresh
orange juice
10 sheets leaf gelatine
50g/2oz/¼ cup sugar
handful of fresh mint leaves, chopped
Limoncello liqueur, for drizzling

COOK'S TIP

The orange juice should be
freshly squeezed if possible.
If you can't freshly sqeeze
your own orange juice, do
try and use the best quality,
freshly squeezed version you
can buy.

PER PORTION Energy 151kcal/641kJ; Protein 9.5g;
Carbohydrate 29.6g, of which sugars 29.6g; Fat 0.2g,
of which saturates 0g; Cholesterol 0mg;
Calcium 26mg; Fibre 0.2g; Sodium 20mg.

SICILIAN ORANGE JELLY
GELO D'AGRUMI

Sicilians love the silky coolness of jelly on a hot summer's day and make it with
all sorts of flavourings, including spices such as cinnamon or the creamy milk
of fresh almonds. For this version, use freshly squeezed orange juice if you have
the time and facilities to squeeze it and serve the dessert in pretty stemmed glasses
so that the light can shine through the gorgeous golden colours of the jelly under
the scattering of deep green mint.

1 Put the orange juice in a pan. Soak the
gelatine in a small bowl of cold water for
5 minutes or until floppy, then drain, squeeze
and add it to the juice.

2 Add the sugar. Stir vigorously over low heat
until the sugar has dissolved and the gelatine
has melted completely.

3 Pour into a shallow square or rectangular
mould. Chill until firm.

4 Remove the set jelly from the refrigerator,
and cut into rough cubes.

5 Arrange in four stemmed glasses, scatter
with the mint leaves and drizzle with Limoncello.

CALABRIAN FROZEN NOUGAT
TORRONE GELATO

This extremely sweet dessert is best served with chilled semi-sweet white wine. It is not real nougat, but a variation on the theme. Making it takes skill and requires the use of a loaf tin or terrine, but the final result looks so spectacular that the effort is certainly worthwhile. It is important to use good-quality candied fruit.
In Calabria, candied fruit nearly always includes thick pieces of the locally grown limes, oranges and tangerines, and is very special.

1 Line a 1.3kg/3lb loaf tin (pan) or several smaller tins with clear film (plastic wrap), leaving plenty of overhang. Grease with almond oil.

2 Put the icing sugar in a large bowl. Stir in just enough lemon juice to make a mixture that resembles dough. It should be neither runny nor hard, but malleable enough to be kneaded.

3 Divide the mixture into three equal parts. Knead the lemon essence into the first part, the red colouring into the second part and the cocoa into the third, making sure that the colourings and flavourings are evenly distributed in each case.

4 Mix the almonds and candied fruit in a bowl. Divide the mixture into three parts and add one part to each quantity of sugar paste.

5 Add one of the pieces of sugar paste to the tin and press it down to form an even layer. Mould the second piece of paste to the shape of the tin and press it evenly on top of the first layer. Top with the third layer of sugar paste.

6 Bring the surplus clear film lining over the paste to enclose it and add a weight to compress the moulded mixture evenly. Chill in the refrigerator for 3 days.

7 Put the chocolate in a heatproof bowl over a small pan of boiling water. Immediately remove from the heat and leave for 5 minutes or until the chocolate has melted, stirring occasionally.

8 Remove the weight from the mould, unfold the covering, invert it on a board and unwrap it. Thickly spread the melted chocolate over the mould and chill until hard. Serve in thin slices.

SERVES 24

1kg/2¼lb/9 cups icing (confectioners') sugar, sifted
juice of 1 or 2 lemons (see Cook's Tip)
3 drops lemon essence (extract)
3 drops red food colouring
25g/1oz/4 tbsp unsweetened cocoa powder
50g/2oz/½ cup blanched almonds, roughly chopped
275g/10oz/2 cups assorted candied fruit, roughly chopped
225g/8oz dark (bittersweet) chocolate, broken into pieces
almond oil for greasing

COOK'S TIP

Lemons vary considerably in size and in the amount of juice they contain. Use just enough to make a malleable paste. To spread the paste in the pan or mould, use a metal spoon dipped in boiling water.

PER PORTION Energy 230kcal/974kJ; Protein 1.2g; Carbohydrate 51.4g, of which sugars 50.3g; Fat 3.5g, of which saturates 1.8g; Cholesterol 1mg; Calcium 30mg; Fibre 0.4g; Sodium 14mg.

SICILIAN WATERMELON ICE
GELATO DI COCOMERO

Nowhere in the world will you taste ice creams and water ices quite like those produced in Sicily, and the following recipe, with its intense perfume and flavour, is a superb example. Do make sure you use a really sweet, ripe watermelon; in Sicily their perfume wafts on the breeze throughout the summer.

1 Press the watermelon through a sieve (strainer) into a bowl.

2 Add half the sugar and stir until dissolved, then mix in the jasmine flower or orange blossom water.

3 Scrape the mixture into a mould or freezerproof bowl and freeze, stirring every 10 minutes or so to break up the ice crystals.

4 When the mixture is thick and slushy, stir in the remaining sugar, then the chocolate, nuts, pumpkin and cinnamon.

5 Return the mould or bowl to the freezer and continue to freeze until the mixture is solid, stirring occasionally.

6 To serve, dip the mould briefly into hot water to loosen the edges. Spoon into serving dishes.

SERVES 6 TO 8

500g/1¼lb watermelon, seeded
  and skinned
275g/10oz/1¼ cups caster
  (superfine) sugar
30ml/2 tbsp jasmine flower water or
  10ml/2 tsp orange blossom water
115g/4oz dark (bittersweet)
  chocolate, diced
40g/1½oz/3 tbsp hulled and
  skinned pistachio nuts, chopped
115g/4oz/⅔ cup candied
  pumpkin, diced
5ml/1 tsp ground cinnamon

COOK'S TIP

Candied pumpkin is very common all over Sicily and is widely available in all good Italian food shops elsewhere. A good alternative would be candied pear as it shares a similar texture and appearance.

PER PORTION Energy 294kcal/1243kJ; Protein 2.1g; Carbohydrate 58.6g, of which sugars 57.7g; Fat 7.3g, of which saturates 2.9g; Cholesterol 1mg; Calcium 52mg; Fibre 1.1g; Sodium 72mg.

INDEX

PUBLISHER'S ACKNOWLEDGEMENTS
The publishers would like to thank the
following for permission to reproduce
their images (t = top, b = bottom, l = left
and r = right): p7tl Sandro Vannini/Corbis,
p7tr Franz-Marc Frei/Corbis; p7br David
Lyons/Alamy; p8bl Byzantine School,
Bridgeman Art Library; p8br Stefano
Bianchetti/Corbis; p9 Terry Harris Just
Greece Photo Library/Alamy; p10, p13bl,
15tl, 15tr CuboImages srl/Alamy; p11bl
Cephas Picture Library/Alamy; p11tr
Lightworks Media/Alamy; p12 Vito
Arcamano/Alamy; 13br Hemis/Alamy;
14bl Gianni Muratore/Alamy; 14br
photosublime/Alamy; p46r, p50r, p54r,
p57l, p72r, p80r, p90r, p98r, p102r, p117l,
p118r, p121l iStockphoto.com